BRITISH
PRIME MINISTERS

BRITISH
PRIME MINISTERS

ROBERT J. PARKER

AMBERLEY

This edition first published 2013

Amberley Publishing
The Hill, Stroud
Gloucestershire, GL5 4EP

www.amberleybooks.com

British Library Cataloguing in Publication Data.
A catalogue record for this book is available from the British Library.

ISBN 978-1-4456-1021-4

Typesetting and Origination by Amberley Publishing.
Printed and bound in Great Britain by
Marston Book Services Ltd, Oxfordshire

CONTENTS

PREFACE

During frequent visits to the United Kingdom, I became aware of a seeming vacuum of information on the former Prime Ministers of Great Britain. As an American who had grown up with a wealth of available information about the US presidents, I was surprised by the lack of data on many of Britain's former leaders. There were countless guides concerning the monarchs and thick single-volume biographies of famous PMs such as Pitt, Gladstone, and Churchill. But who were the rest?

My first endeavour was to travel around Great Britain identifying their gravesites – an enjoyable but formidable task since there was no single source that gave all their final resting places. This led me to the conclusion that a brief work, identifying and describing all fifty-three British Prime Ministers and their burial locations (where relevant), would provide a useful and worthwhile source of reference and entertainment, for both visitors to Britain and UK citizens alike.

Personally, I have found delving into the background of these fifty-two men and one woman to be a fascinating journey. I hope that these brief glimpses into the lives and times of these leaders will spur you to probe more deeply into those personalities which you find most intriguing and, perhaps, introduce you to those of whom you were not previously aware.

Robert J. Parker
Valparaiso, Indiana, March 2011

INTRODUCTION

The modern position of Prime Minister in the United Kingdom has evolved over several centuries. It is an extension of the parliamentary system of government, a system that has become the most popular form of democratic government in the world today. The prototype of all parliamentary governments is that of England. It emerged from noble barons demanding that the monarch seek their approval in certain circumstances: this was the basis of Magna Carta in 1215. It was followed by the establishment of a 'speaking place' for representatives of noble birth and various towns: this was Parliament. The institution evolved under King Henry III in the thirteenth century and later under Edward III in the fourteenth century, splitting into separate houses for nobility (Lords) and knights and burgesses (Commons). For several centuries a tug of war ensued between the monarch and Parliament. The struggle generally revolved around who should control the power of the purse, which provided or denied the monarch the wherewithal to pursue wars, grand projects, or a lavish lifestyle.

All monarchs had senior advisors, or ministers, to carry out the various functions of government. Some would inevitably become powerful and dominant figures within the kingdom. This enviable position had its rewards, but also its risks, as evidenced by Henry VIII's treatment of Cardinal Wolsey (who would surely have faced execution had he not died first), and the executions of fallen chief ministers Thomas More and Thomas Cromwell. Later ministers such as William Cecil, and his son Robert, made enormous contributions to the reigns of Elizabeth I and James I, but although they were indeed loyal, trusted, and powerful 'chief ministers', they do not quite adhere to our later definition of 'Prime Minister'.

The English Civil War during the reign of Charles I, and the rise of Parliament's strong leader, Oliver Cromwell, as Lord Protector (which saw the country's only experience of republic), demonstrated that Parliament had gained powers it would never relinquish. The restoration of the monarchy in 1660 under Charles II, followed by the relatively peaceful removal of his brother James II in 1688, emphasised that *all* future monarchs would be forced to acknowledge the will of Parliament, its consent in their wearing of the crown, and its control of the purse strings.

The selection in 1714 of George I from the German state of Hanover further increased the necessity for the King to work with Parliament in order to achieve any kind of productive policy. Being very German and speaking little English, George relied upon the leader of Parliament, Sir Robert Walpole, to also serve as his chief advisor. The combination of these two powerful positions saw the birth of what is now known as the office of Prime Minister. Walpole maintained this position from 1721 to 1742. He used his control of parliamentary legislation, patronage, and the assumption of the post of First Lord of the Treasury, to control the setting and funding of the political agenda. The blending of parliamentary leader with the office of First Lord of the Treasury would become the hallmark of future Prime Ministers.

However, the title and trappings of the highest office in the land have not been recognised by all its holders. The occupancy of an official residence at No. 10 Downing Street began with Walpole, but not all PMs have lived there. Many early holders of the top job objected to the title of 'Prime Minister'; indeed, it was not used officially until 1878. And only in 1905 did King Edward VII begin to introduce the Prime Minister in official order of precedence at formal gatherings.

Originally, the monarch had a large hand in the selection and acceptance of the person assuming the post, as the sovereign was the supreme leader of the nation and head of state (and technically the monarch remains head of state in the United Kingdom and must formally invite a new Prime Minister to form a government). But gradually it became clear that the real power in the nation was to be entrusted to an elected legislature and its recognisable, accountable leader.

Today, though not quite 'presidential', the Prime Minister is certainly 'premier', providing representation for the UK on the world stage, directing the government's foreign and domestic policy, steering legislation through Parliament, and making key speeches on important issues. Along with the monarch, the Prime Minister is, for the rest of the world, the identifiable face of the United Kingdom.

A BRIEF OVERVIEW OF
BRITISH POLITICAL PARTIES

The following is a very brief overview of the political designations that became attached to Members of Parliament and Prime Ministers. While originally fluid and informal, party affiliation gradually gained greater acceptance and discipline, eventually evolving into the modern party identities of today.

Whigs

The name 'Whig' derives from the Scottish 'whiggamore' and was essentially applied to those who opposed absolute monarchy. The Whigs supported George I, the Hanoverian monarch who was brought in from the German state in 1714, and opposed those who favoured restoration of the Catholic Stuart dynasty and later the 'Young Pretender', Bonnie Prince Charlie. The origin of the Whigs is normally given as 1688 and the 'Glorious Revolution' of that year, which saw the removal of James II from the throne.

By the time of Sir Robert Walpole and the birth of what we now know as the post of 'Prime Minister', the Whigs were firmly entrenched as the leading political organisation in Parliament. Until midway through the nineteenth century, Whigs supported aristocratic families, Catholic emancipation, broader suffrage rights, and the abolition of slavery. The Whigs would eventually split over reform issues, free trade, and the Irish question, combining with reform-minded Tory Party members to form the Liberal Party. They ceased to be a viable political force by the late nineteenth century.

Tories

'Tory' is today used to describe members of the modern Conservative Party. Originally, the Tories were those who firmly supported the monarchy. Accused of opposing the removal of James II during the 'Glorious Revolution' of 1688, the 'new' Tories did not re-emerge until the end of the eighteenth century under King George III. Led by William Pitt (the Younger), Tories challenged the radical politics of the French Revolution and Napoleon, but were no more supportive of the Crown than the Whigs. During the mid-nineteenth century, the party split over the issue of free trade. The more reform-minded members merged with like-minded Whigs to form the Liberal Party, while Robert Peel led his 'Peelite' wing in the formation of what was to become a new 'Conservative' party. The Tory Party ceased to exist, although the nickname 'Tory' has been applied to the Conservative Party up to the present day.

Liberals

Formed in the mid-nineteenth century by reform-minded elements of the Whig and Tory Parties, the Liberals favoured free trade, extension of the franchise, and a reduction of Crown powers. The Liberal Party featured the determined leadership of dynamic social reformers such as William Gladstone in the late nineteenth century and Herbert Asquith in the early twentieth. However, the First World War and the Great Depression presented formidable challenges that helped to relegate the Liberal Party to virtual obscurity as the Labour Party superseded it as the most popular progressive force in British politics. The party's fortunes were improved in the late twentieth century by joining with the Social Democratic Party (SDP) to form the Liberal Democrats in 1988.

Conservatives

In 1834, Robert Peel issued the Tamworth Manifesto proclaiming the goals of his wing ('Peelites') of the Tory Party. This grouping was to emerge as the new Conservative Party, the Tory Party having split over issues of free trade and social reform. Further definition of Conservative philosophy was projected through the leadership of nineteenth-century Conservative Prime Ministers, namely Edward Smith-Stanley (Earl of Derby) and Benjamin Disraeli. More often in government than not during the troubled twentieth century, the Conservative Party remains to this day the major force on the right of British politics.

Labour

The Labour Party traces its founding to 1900, when left-wing organisations collaborated to seek stronger representation in Parliament for the working class. A founder member and the party's first leader was Keir Hardie, the Scottish socialist. A complex set of causes contributed to the decline of the Liberal Party and the rise of Labour after the First World War, and in 1924 Ramsay MacDonald, another Scot, became the party's first Prime Minister. The Labour Party originally claimed to represent the interests of trade unions and the mass of ordinary workers, and was heavily influenced by socialist thought; yet in recent years – especially since the period of New Labour under Tony Blair – the party has increasingly distanced itself from the trade unions, staking out the centre ground of British politics and aiming to appeal to as broad a base as possible. In spite of New Labour's faltering in the early twenty-first century, the Labour Party continues to be a significant political movement in the United Kingdom.

Liberal Democrats

A merging of the Liberal Party and Social Democrats, the Liberal Democrats officially formed in 1988. Disenchanted parliamentary members of the Labour Party combined with what had become a small and marginal Liberal Party to create a political and ideological alternative to the two main parties. The Liberal Democrats have succeeded in getting members elected to Parliament but have yet to develop a large enough base to produce a Prime Minister. In 2010, however, they aligned with the Conservatives to form a coalition government – the first coalition government since the Second World War. In supporting Conservative Prime Minister David Cameron, the Lib-Dems achieved Cabinet representation for the first time, which saw party leader Nick Clegg appointed as Deputy Prime Minister.

SIR ROBERT WALPOLE

Born: 26 August 1676
Died: 18 March 1745
Party: Whig
Served: 4 April 1721 – 11 February 1742
(20 years, 314 days)

"My great crime is my long continuance in office, and the exclusion of those who now complain against me"

SIR ROBERT WALPOLE is generally recognised as the first Prime Minister of Great Britain. Certainly there were many 'prime' or essential ministers to the various monarchs of England, but by the eighteenth century the power of Parliament in relation to the monarch, coupled with the duty and ability to lead Parliament, was increasingly invested in one man. Since the dominant question was usually that of money, the position of First Lord of the Treasury became the seat of power. The monarch's desire to control policy required the corresponding approval of Parliament in order to finance any kind of programme, either domestic or foreign. This in turn necessitated a ministerial position that would persuade Parliament to fund the monarch's desires. This 'Prime Minister' would be more than the monarch's advisor – he would become the conduit for obtaining the means to implement the monarch's desired policy. Eventually, this policy would become more and more the Prime Minister's policy, representing the wishes of Parliament and the constituencies that elected it.

Sir Robert Walpole grasped this concept and established himself as Great Britain's leading politician for nearly four decades. By catering to the King on a personal advisory level, and by manipulating the national purse through the control of Parliament and the office of the Treasury, Walpole became the foremost instrument of policy, finance, and patronage. His ability to control and distribute these three key sources of power provided him with the leverage to dominate British politics at home and abroad. More than that, it inaugurated the office that was to eclipse the power of the throne, helping to create the modern system of democratically elected representative government that has become the basic standard for parliamentary governments around the world today.

Walpole was the third son of Robert and Mary (*née* Burwell) Walpole. He was educated at Eton and Cambridge, and became heir to the Walpole estates at Houghton, Norfolk following the deaths of his elder brothers. Walpole first entered Parliament in 1701 where he gained advantageous patronage from the influential Churchills (the Duke and Duchess of Marlborough). He rose swiftly in lucrative government positions, but was sent to the Tower of London in 1712 on charges of corruption – charges that were largely the result of his then out-of-favour Whig political persuasion. Party identification was growing at this time, with Whigs and Tories emerging as the two largest and most readily distinguished labels of affiliation.

The death of Queen Anne in 1714, and the arrival of the first king of the House of Hanover, George I, brought Walpole and the Whigs back into power. Walpole consolidated his position with the new monarch through his control of Parliament and his tenure of the office of First Lord of the Treasury. This combination became the hallmark that was to define a Prime Minister.

From 1721 to 1742, Walpole established the agenda and oversaw the running of government. His fundamental principles were simple and sound: low taxes, avoidance of war to keep expenses in check, and political stability within his Whig-controlled Parliament. When George I died in 1727, Walpole expected to be replaced. The former Prince of Wales, now George II, was not fond of Walpole, but no immediate or adequate replacement presented himself so Walpole remained in power.

He maintained his position until the ravages of ill health, advanced age, and an unwanted war with Spain finally took their toll. As his control over Parliament gradually declined, the number of his political enemies increased. Those who had either lost or been denied positions of influence now sought his removal. He resigned his position as First Lord of the Treasury in 1742, effectively ending his premiership.

Besides accruing power, Walpole had also acquired an immense fortune. He built a splendid palatial manor house at Houghton, purchased a fabulous art collection (later sold to the Empress of Russia, Catherine the Great, and on display at the Hermitage Museum in St Petersburg), and became one of the last of Britain's 'chief' ministers to acquire a fortune through the shrewd use of their position. He became Knight of the Bath in 1725, Knight of the Garter in 1726, and Earl of Orford in 1742. George II offered Walpole the house at No. 10 Downing Street in order to be within walking distance of Parliament. Walpole declined ownership but lived in this residence as the First Lord of the Treasury. After more than two and a half centuries, it remains the official and iconic residence of the Prime Minister.

Walpole married Catherine Shorter in 1700, and though mainly living apart, this unhappy marriage did produce six children, including the well-known writer Horace Walpole. When his first wife died in 1737, Walpole married his long-time lover, Maria Skerrett, but she died in the same year of their marriage, 1738.

Walpole was known for his coarse ways and unclean clothing. He may or may not have said 'Every man has his price', but the attribution is hardly unfair if he didn't. He died in London in 1745, and is buried in St Martin's church, located in the grounds of his magnificent manor house, Houghton Hall, in Norfolk.

SPENCER COMPTON

EARL OF WILMINGTON

Born: *c.* 18 March 1673
Died: 2 July 1743
Party: Whig
Served: 16 February 1742 – 2 July 1743
         (1 year, 136 days)

*"Sir, you have the right to speak,
but the House has the right to
judge whether they hear you"
(to the Duke of Newcastle)*

SPENCER COMPTON, 1st Earl of Wilmington, was Britain's second acknowledged Prime Minister. For more than two decades the powerful Sir Robert Walpole had dominated British politics. Eventually there developed an increasing climate for political change. The ensuing competition for Walpole's replacement ended in Spencer Compton's emergence as the new First Lord of the Treasury, and with that key appointment he became heir to Walpole's role as Prime Minister. He would serve King George II from February 1742 until his death in July 1743.

Compton was born the second son to the 3rd Earl of Northampton, James Compton, and his wife Mary (*née* Noel, daughter of the 3rd Viscount Campden). Educated at Trinity College, Oxford, Compton took up the practice of law and also entered politics. His upbringing had been strongly Royalist Tory, but in Parliament he skilfully aligned with the Whigs under Walpole. Compton held several important positions under Walpole, including Speaker of the House and Paymaster General of the Army. Holding these powerful offices enabled Compton to build a reputation for being highly skilled in parliamentary procedure and to accumulate a sizeable personal fortune.

He adroitly endeared himself to the future king, the then Prince of Wales, and in 1727, with the death of George I, the new king George II sought a change in government. It is believed that Compton was the choice he had in mind. For whatever reason – fear, greed, lack of ambition, or a combination – Compton declined the premiership, choosing instead to remain a loyal supporting administrator to Walpole's leadership. In return for this dedicated support, Compton was rewarded with an earldom. Walpole remained in charge for another fifteen years while Compton waited in the wings.

In 1742, when Walpole's lengthy tenure finally collapsed, Compton emerged as the leader of a group of contenders that included several powerful Whigs: William Pulteney, John (Lord) Carteret, and Henry Pelham. Pelham and his faction were squeezed out, allowing Compton, Carteret and Pulteney to claim and divide the spoils of high office. Compton took on the role of First Lord of the Treasury and effectively became Britain's second Prime Minister.

Compton left much of the important decision-making to Lord Carteret, which was their agreement and intention all along as Compton was weak with illness and never comfortable with the weight of heavy responsibility. He died in office on 2 July 1743. Because he was unmarried and had no legitimate heirs, his large fortune was left to his nephew, the 5th Earl of Northampton. The cities of Wilmington in the US states of Delaware and North Carolina are named after him. He is buried unmarked in the crypt of the family church on the Northampton estate of Compton Wynyates, Warwickshire. Compton's tomb is one of the few prime ministerial burial sites in private grounds and is closed to the public.

George II (reigned 1727–60).

HENRY PELHAM

Born: 25 September 1694
Died: 6 March 1754
Party: Whig
Served: 27 August 1743 – 6 March 1754
            (10 years, 191 days)

*"The House of Commons is a great
unwieldy body, which requires
great art and some cordial
to keep it loyal"*

HENRY PELHAM served as Prime Minister under King George II from August 1743 until his death in office in March 1754. Following Pelham's death, his brother Thomas Pelham-Holles, Duke of Newcastle, would become the next Prime Minister – making them the only brothers (so far) to hold the premiership. Henry Pelham was strongly supported by Sir Robert Walpole, the still-powerful former PM, ensuring continued Whig Party dominance of British government.

Pelham had been groomed by Walpole, and was dubbed his 'chief clerk'. He was edged out of becoming Prime Minister after Walpole's fall from power in 1742, but with the death of the pedestrian Spencer Compton in 1743, Pelham became First Lord of the Treasury and embarked upon a decade of competent, if hardly spectacular, leadership. Notably, there was a fifty-six-day gap between the death of Compton and the selection of Henry Pelham, the longest such gap to this day for Prime Ministers in the post-Walpole era.

Pelham's brother, the Duke of Newcastle, controlled a large power bloc in Parliament, providing the necessary voting muscle to retain Whig control, pass legislation, and conduct policy. Pelham was able to conclude the expensive and indecisive War of Austrian Succession (1748), adopt the Gregorian calendar for Britain (instituted elsewhere as early as 1582), and put down the Jacobite uprising of Bonnie Prince Charlie at the Battle of Culloden (1746). Pelham also insisted, against the King's wishes, that the dynamic and energetic William Pitt be brought into the government. Pitt's appointment and presence was to have a far-reaching impact upon the government, England, and indeed the world at large. Eventually, George II grew to have great faith in and reliance upon Pelham, and was deeply troubled by his death in office, proclaiming 'Now I shall have no more peace.'

Henry Pelham was born in 1695, the second son of Thomas Pelham and Lady Grace Holles, and educated at Oxford and Padua, Italy. He served briefly in the British Army before representing Seaford, and later Sussex, in Parliament. Married in 1726 to Lady Katherine Manners, daughter of the 2nd Duke of Rutland, Henry fathered six daughters and two sons – but both sons died in 1739 of a sore throat condition that became known as 'Pelham's disease'. Pelham worked his way up gradually through several important ministerial posts under the watchful eye and guidance of his mentor Sir Robert Walpole. Pelham's wealthy brother, the Duke of Newcastle, provided the necessary financial fuel for their political aspirations, while Pelham displayed the greater gift for politics and superior social skills. Together, they were a potent combination.

Pelham's decade in power featured strong commitments to fiscal responsibility, reduction of land taxes and national debt, and a determination in all matters to conduct a policy of stability. Indeed, it is stability and integrity that are usually associated with Henry Pelham. He died in London, while still in office, on 6 March 1754, and is buried beside his brother (and successor as Prime Minister) in All Saints church, Laughton, East Sussex.

'The Beheading of the Rebel Lords on Great Tower Hill'. The leaders of the Jacobite Rebellion are executed in 1746 following their defeat at the Battle of Culloden.

THOMAS PELHAM-HOLLES

DUKE OF NEWCASTLE

Born:	21 July 1693
Died:	17 November 1768
Party:	Whig
Served:	16 March 1754 – 16 November 1756
	2 July 1757 – 26 May 1762
	(7 years, 205 days)

"I shall not think the demands of the people a rule of conduct, nor shall I ever fear to incur their resentment in the prosecution of their interest"

THOMAS PELHAM-HOLLES, the 1st Duke of Newcastle (or simply Newcastle for short), held the office of Prime Minister twice: he replaced his deceased brother, Henry Pelham, from 1754 to 1756, and he served again between 1757 and 1762. Henry and Thomas Pelham remain so far the only brothers to serve as Prime Minister. Thomas Pelham-Holles' premierships overlapped the end of George II's reign and the start of George III's, and were deeply influenced by the participation of William Pitt, who was a virtual co-premier. Pitt filled a key role in Newcastle's administration, just as Newcastle had filled one in his brother's government

Thomas Pelham was born in 1693, the eldest son of Thomas Pelham (1st Baron Pelham) and his second wife, Lady Grace Holles, sister of John Holles, Duke of Newcastle. He was educated at Cambridge, adopted by his uncle in 1711 (adding the name Holles to inherit his estate), and made Duke of Newcastle-upon-Tyne in 1715. For the next five decades, encompassing the reigns of three kings, Newcastle rendered service at numerous levels of government. His enormous wealth provided the parliamentary foundation for decades of Whig power. It was said that he was the greatest borough-buyer of his time and that he always knew the cost of any vote in the House of Commons. Unfortunately, his skill in securing the necessary votes was at odds with his personality and inability to manage an effective administration. He admirably assisted the governments of Walpole and Henry Pelham, but relied heavily upon Pitt to co-ordinate his own premiership. It was an odd contrast, for a most odd man.

An extreme hypochondriac, Newcastle exhibited an almost neurotic fear of catching colds and had a tendency to faint and break down into public fits of weeping, gaining him an almost comical reputation among most observers. His social skills were peculiar at best, embarrassing at worst, and noted by a wide spectrum of commentators, friends and enemies alike. It was evident to all that Newcastle, though a vital and energetic member of the Whig leadership, was short on the qualities needed to conduct an effective administration on his own. In concert with others, however, Newcastle provided continuous and positive service.

His first term as premier saw Britain engaged in a major war with France. The loss of the Mediterranean island of Minorca and the defeat of British armies to the French in North America, plus the departure of several essential ministers including Henry Fox and William Pitt, underscored Newcastle's failure to maintain an effective government and brought about his resignation in 1756. The Whigs, however, maintained power under the temporary leadership of William Cavendish, Duke of Devonshire, and were ably supported by the political brilliance and enthusiasm of Pitt, so that by 1757 Newcastle was back in power again, albeit with Pitt as the primary policy maker.

With Pitt as Secretary of State and Fox as Paymaster General, Newcastle presided over an uneasy but highly successful alliance during the Seven Years' War (1756–63). Pitt's genius in crafting global strategy toward India, North America, and control of the oceans, brought Britain to unprecedented heights of success. The birth of Great Britain's mighty world empire began with the dramatic and simultaneous conquests of far-flung territories tethered by a navy of unparalleled size and strength.

Under the surface of these great successes came increased criticism and opposition from George III and his Tory followers led by John Stuart (Lord Bute). Straining beneath royal pressure, Newcastle could not hold his government together. Pitt resigned in 1761, Newcastle followed in May 1762, and the era of 'old' Whig domination came to an end.

Newcastle married Lady Henrietta Godolphin in 1717, but they had no children. He died in November 1768. Though riddled with character and leadership flaws, Newcastle provided important contributions to Britain's imperial achievements. Easy to ridicule, he is also difficult to dismiss. He lies buried beside his brother Henry, the two Prime Ministers together, in All Saints church, Laughton, East Sussex.

WILLIAM CAVENDISH

DUKE OF DEVONSHIRE

Born:	8 May 1720
Died:	2 October 1764
Party:	Whig
Served:	16 November 1756 – 25 June 1757
	(225 days)

"Every king must make use of human means to attain human ends or his affairs will go to ruin"

WILLIAM CAVENDISH, the 4th Duke of Devonshire, was Prime Minister under King George II from November 1756 to July 1757. He was born the eldest son of William Cavendish, the 3rd Duke of Devonshire, and Catherine Hoskins. His father was a close friend and strong Whig Party ally of Sir Robert Walpole. The younger Cavendish was tutored at home, went on a Grand Tour of Europe, and entered politics as a Whig Member of Parliament from Derbyshire. In 1748 he married Charlotte Boyle, Baroness Clifford and the heiress of the Earl of Burlington and Cork. Through this marriage Cavendish acquired vast estates in Yorkshire and Ireland. He became the 4th Duke of Devonshire upon the death of his father in 1756. He and his wife had three sons and one daughter. The daughter, Lady Dorothy, married William Bentinck, 3rd Duke of Portland and twice Prime Minister (1783 and 1807–09).

Devonshire's tenure in office was short, only nine months, and was brought about by the political infighting between George II and the factions of the Whig Party led by William Pitt and the Duke of Newcastle. The King wanted nothing to do with William Pitt and was desperate to be rid of him. Newcastle, as Prime Minister, was willing to sacrifice Pitt, but Pitt's considerable following in Parliament remained essential to the government. In fact, William Pitt, as Secretary of State, was already conducting not only foreign affairs, but also the majority of the other duties of government, even though Newcastle was officially in charge as First Lord of the Treasury. Something had to give in this three-way waltz. Newcastle resigned on the understanding that Devonshire, who was acceptable to the King, would take over as Prime Minister. This satisfied the Whigs since, in essence, even though Devonshire had the title, Pitt would retain the power. This merry sham infuriated the King, who eventually found an excuse (the Admiral Byng affair) to sack Pitt.

For his part, Devonshire was willing to comply because of his loyalty to the King, his commitment to harmony among the Whigs, and the fact that England was preparing to engage France in the Seven Years' War. There was important work to do and Devonshire understood the need to get on with it. Admiral Byng, who was accused of cowardice and blamed for the loss of Minorca to the French, was sentenced to death. Pitt argued for Byng's innocence, but public opinion and the King demanded punishment. To the King's delight, Pitt resigned over the issue and Devonshire had Byng executed. Pitt and Newcastle eventually patched up their differences, Devonshire resigned, Newcastle returned as Prime Minister with Pitt again as Secretary of State and virtual premier, and the whole show had now come full circle. For his troubles, Devonshire was appointed Lord Chamberlain, a position he relished and enjoyed until 1762, when he was dismissed by the new king, George III.

The Devonshire family estate at Chatsworth is one of Britain's great manor house properties, not least because Cavendish hired Lancelot 'Capability' Brown to landscape the extensive park and gardens. William Cavendish died of dropsy in 1764 in what is today Spa in Belgium, the only Prime Minister to die on foreign soil. He is buried in the Cavendish family vault in Derby Cathedral.

Chatsworth, the Devonshire family estate.

JOHN STUART

EARL OF BUTE

Born:	25 May 1713
Died:	10 March 1792
Party:	Tory
Served:	26 May 1762 – 8 April 1763
	(317 days)

"If I had but £50 per annum I would retire and think it a luxury compared with what I suffer"

JOHN STUART, the 3rd Earl of Bute, served as Prime Minister under King George III from May 1762 until April 1763. His short-lived premiership drew deep resentment from both politicians and populace. Bute's accession to high office and political prominence was propelled entirely by his close association with the royal family, as he was basically devoid of any political experience, intuition, or even aspiration. Bute's background, ideas, and policies pleased virtually no one except the King, at whose pleasure he served.

John Stuart was the son of James Stuart, the 2nd Earl of Bute, and Lady Anne Campbell, daughter of the 1st Duke of Argyle. Born in Edinburgh and educated at Eton, Stuart assumed the earldom on the death of his father in 1723. In 1736, he married the wealthy Mary Wortley Montagu, and upon her father's death in 1761 Bute assumed control of her inherited fortune. Bute showed little early interest in politics, preferring instead to tend his Scottish estates while studying botany and architecture. Socially active, he was known for his handsome features and what were described as the 'best legs in London'. While living in the capital, Bute met the Prince and Princess of Wales, with whom he became quite close. Upon Prince Frederick's early death in 1751, Bute was entrusted with the tutoring of the widowed Princess's son, Prince George.

Bute took the development of the young Prince George quite seriously, becoming the closest and dearest advisor to both the Prince and his mother Augusta. When the Prince became King George III in 1760, it was to John Stuart that he turned for advice and support. To this end Bute was devoted, dedicated, and displayed no little skill. George III's first order of business was ending the expensive Seven Years' War with

France. The King and Bute were determined to end it immediately, though Secretary of State William Pitt was all for expanding the war by attacking Spain to further increase and secure Britain's overseas interests. The rejection of this policy and subsequent resignations by Pitt and the Whig Prime Minister Henry Pelham-Holles (Duke of Newcastle) offered George III the opportunity to engineer the appointment of Bute as First Lord of the Treasury, allowing him to form a new government as Prime Minister.

Bute did achieve some success. The Treaty of Paris was successfully negotiated with France in 1763, adding enormous amounts of colonial territory to the British Empire while ending the exorbitant demands of fighting what amounted to a global war. Bute then began the reduction of Whig political power by weeding out members of the Whig administration, a pruning that became known as the 'massacre of the Pelham innocents'. This purge of the 'old' Whig power structure was a keen desire of George III, and though Bute was able to carry this out, it was at the price of his and the King's already sagging popularity. When Bute attempted to introduce a cider tax in order to help pay war debts, his unpopularity provoked dangerously violent reactions and threats.

The pushing through of the cider tax, coupled with the furore over his removal of the 'old' Whigs, signalled Bute's determination to carry out the King's policy even if it proved to be his political undoing. Everything about Bute soon came under withering attack, from his Scottish background to his relationship with the Princess of Wales, with whom he was frequently accused of having an affair. Even after his resignation, Bute was mercilessly criticised for continuing to privately advise the King. The next Prime Minister, George Grenville, insisted that Bute be completely removed from court, and he finally was in September 1763.

Bute retreated to his estates and played little further role in politics, devoting his time to books, botany, and the raising of his eleven children. Yet the contempt for Bute was so severe that, six years later in 1769, his London house was attacked by a mob, and as late as 1771 he and Princess Augusta were still being hanged and burned in effigy. To say that Bute became disenchanted by politics would be an understatement. Yet although roundly disparaged in his own time, many modern historians give Bute much credit for negotiating a successful end to the Seven Years' War.

He died in London in 1792 and is buried in the Bute family tomb outside the 'Old Kirk' church, Rothesay, Isle of Bute, Scotland.

GEORGE GRENVILLE

Born: 14 October 1712
Died: 13 November 1770
Party: Whig
Served: 16 April 1763 – 13 July 1765
           (2 years, 85 days)

"A wise government knows how to enforce with temper, or to conciliate with dignity"

GEORGE GRENVILLE served as Prime Minister under King George III, from 1763 to 1765. Grenville's strengths were his integrity, devotion to efficient government, and dedication to paying off the national debt incurred during the enormously expensive Seven Years' War. His fiscal responsibility would become one of the defining legacies of his premiership. This dedication led to an imaginative colonial taxation scheme, the infamous Stamp Act, which would provoke the thirteen North American colonies into a state of rebellion and eventually spawn a newly independent United States of America.

Grenville was born in 1712, the second son of the politically well-connected Richard and Hester (*née* Temple) Grenville. After an education at Eton and Oxford, Grenville pursued a career in politics and soon rose through the ranks of Parliament and several ministerial positions including Lord of the Treasury, Treasurer of the Navy, and Secretary of State.

Grenville was involved in several areas of reform. He was opposed to the use of 'press gangs' to force unwilling seamen into the Navy, and he reformed the payment of sailors by eliminating an unfair and fraudulent voucher system. As Prime Minister, he believed in relying on a smaller core of faithful Cabinet members to assist his decision-making, more closely resembling today's centralised model of operating an executive branch.

Of both historical and topical interest is Grenville's reaction to the 'Wilkes Affair'. To the modern mind, his response to this episode in 1763 seems reasoned and level-headed. As a Member of Parliament, John Wilkes was a notoriously vocal and vehement critic of George III. Naturally the King and his supporters felt these attacks to be unjust and irresponsible, and they sought arrest through charges of libel. Wilkes was expelled from Parliament and fled to France to avoid arrest and prosecution. Grenville believed it a matter for the courts to settle. To this day the question of what constitutes the grey area between legal and libellous criticism of government remains hotly debated and contested.

Grenville is probably best remembered as the author of the Stamp Act. Due to his unstinting dedication toward paying off the Seven Years' War debt, he concluded that it was necessary for the North American colonies to begin shouldering some of the tax burden. The colonies had benefited from the removal of the French threat, and for years had been nurtured by either low taxes, or a willingness to forgo enforcement. Grenville was determined to redress this situation by lowering or removing numerous previous taxes and replacing them with a more modest tax upon printed material, documents, periodicals, etc. It would tighten the tax structure, make it more equitable, and encourage colonial participation in helping pay off the debt the mother country had incurred for its colonies' benefit. In this logical conclusion Grenville could not have been more mistaken.

The colonies were prepared to not only protest and refuse to pay, but to boycott all British imports. The effect was devastating. Coupled with the denial of the expected revenue was the loss of income from vital trade. Worse to come was the surge of outrage and indignation that would increasingly unite the colonies. Their arguments against the tax soon ignited an explosive resentment over the lack of political representation in Parliament, and this in turn mushroomed into a desire for complete independence. For the efficient-minded Grenville, none of this could have been predicted or envisioned. But the die was cast, unleashing a chain of events that would lead to the loss of thirteen of Britain's most valuable and previously loyal possessions.

In his private life, Grenville married Elizabeth Wyndham, who bore him five daughters and four sons. His third son, William Wyndham Grenville, would also become Prime Minister (1806–07), giving the Grenvilles the distinction, excepting the Elder and Younger Pitts, of being the only father and son duo to obtain the premiership. Grenville never lived to see the American independence he had unwittingly instigated, dying as he did in 1770. He is buried near the former Grenville estate in the family row of tombs at All Saints church, Wotton Underwood, Buckinghamshire.

CHARLES WATSON-WENTWORTH

MARQUESS OF ROCKINGHAM

Born:	13 May 1730
Died:	1 July 1782
Party:	Whig
Served:	13 July 1765 – 30 July 1766,
	27 March 1782 – 1 July 1782
	(1 year, 113 days)

*"Englishmen, whatever their
local situation may be, know no
obedience to any thing but the laws"*

CHARLES WATSON-WENTWORTH served twice as Prime Minister under King George III. As a high-ranking member of the Whig Party grandees – those who claimed a long, wealthy, and noble lineage – the 2nd Marquess of Rockingham was able to please most of his parliamentary cohort of shared status while not being overly offensive to the King. His premiership on both occasions was mainly a service of practical convenience, attempting to placate the King while not unduly troubling his aristocratic brethren.

Rockingham was born in 1730, the son of Thomas Watson-Wentworth, 1st Marquess, and Lady Mary Finch, daughter of the 7th Earl of Winchilsea. At the age of fifteen he joined the King's brother, the Duke of Cumberland, in putting down the Jacobite Rebellion of 'Bonnie' Prince Charles. The Duke would later remember and reward this act of youthful loyalty. Educated at Westminster School and Cambridge, Rockingham's inheritance provided wealth and political clout for the Whig Party. He received considerable intellectual support from his secretary, the brilliant political philosopher Edmund Burke, and in 1765, upon the recommendation of the Duke of Cumberland, Rockingham gained the post of Prime Minister.

The deteriorating relationship with the American colonies over the question of taxation, underscored by the fierce colonial defiance to the infamous Stamp Act, had brought about the collapse of the government of George Grenville. The Rockingham faction of the Whig Party sought to repeal the Stamp Act and restore harmony with the colonies, though it also insisted upon reasserting parliamentary control over the colonial situation. A weakness of the Rockingham government proved to be its inability to include the powerful and influential William Pitt, who, though supporting the repeal, decided to oppose the Rockingham faction on other issues. Combined with the resignation of several key Cabinet ministers, the Rockingham administration gave way in 1766 to a new government led by Pitt.

Sixteen years later, in March of 1782, when the government of Lord North finally conceded that the war with the American colonies was a doomed enterprise, Rockingham was called upon again to be Prime Minister. He had warned Parliament as early as 1778 that American independence would be the only outcome of the struggle and that reconciliation should begin immediately. The task was to end the war and establish negotiations with the colonies – perhaps to include independence, although that controversial decision had yet to be agreed upon by Rockingham's government. But in poor health, he died on 1 July 1782, just a few months after regaining office. The chore (and blame) of negotiating a peace with the colonies would fall to the next Prime Minister – William Petty, Earl of Shelburne, Rockingham's Home Secretary.

Rockingham was married in 1752 to Mary Bright, but they had no children. His passion for gambling and raising racehorses was well known. He was frequently in ill health and was not known for his speaking ability, but he was acknowledged by all to be honest and he was certainly determined in maintaining a separation between the powers of Parliament and those of the King. This was firmly demonstrated in his second term as Prime Minister, when he insisted that George III accept the inevitability of colonial independence, which the King did, albeit reluctantly.

In South Yorkshire, Rockingham and his father built one of the largest and finest Georgian manor houses in all of Europe. Privately owned for decades, the grounds and gardens are open to the public while restoration on the main house continues. It is often referred to as 'the greatest manor house you have never heard of'.

Due to his sympathy for the American colonial cause there are numerous counties and towns named after Rockingham in the United States, including Rockingham, North Carolina. He is buried in the Strafford family vault at York Minster Cathedral, York.

WILLIAM PITT THE ELDER

EARL OF CHATHAM

Born: 15 November 1708
Died: 11 May 1778
Party: Whig
Served: 30 July 1766 – 14 October 1768
           (2 years, 76 days)

*"Unlimited power is apt to corrupt
the minds of those who possess it"*

WILLIAM PITT, both as a Prime Minister and a political leader in Parliament, helped create a Great Britain that would straddle the globe geographically, economically, and militarily for the better part of two centuries. His foresight and strategic vision went well beyond Sir Robert Walpole's mere grasping for power and position in Britain and on the European continent. Pitt's design was nothing short of global in its concept and execution. Though many others made significant contributions to Britain's imperial success and achievement, to William Pitt must go much of the credit for the dynamic inspiration that led to world supremacy and dominance.

William Pitt was born in 1708, the second son of Robert Pitt and Harriet Villiers, and grandson of Thomas Pitt, a wealthy India trade merchant. Educated at Trinity College, Oxford, Pitt entered the House of Commons in 1735 for the 'rotten' (i.e. electorally corrupt) borough of Old Sarum in Salisbury. He soon allied himself with those who were in opposition to the serving Prime Minister, Sir Robert Walpole, and, by backing Frederick the Prince of Wales, he also made an enemy of King George II. But Pitt's rhetorical skill in parliamentary debate, his influential friends, and his sheer ability to grasp the concept of world affairs, propelled him to success and high office.

Pitt identified several factors that were crucial for world power: the requirement to possess a strong navy in order to extend and protect Britain's power globally; the need to confront France on the global stage and to maintain equality with, if not superiority over, this traditional enemy; and the development of commercial trade on a global basis in order to stimulate the economic growth and vitality of the motherland. Among these central themes, Pitt recognised the enormous economic opportunity created through trade and the acquisition of overseas colonies, both as a means to generate raw materials and as a way of expanding markets. These were powerful ideas in the late eighteenth century, ideas that when fully developed would enable Britain to dominate world trade over the next 150 years.

Pitt was instrumental in Britain's success during the Seven Years' War (1756–63). Serving as Secretary of State for foreign affairs within what was essentially a coalition government, Pitt wielded direct control over the war effort during the administration of Thomas Pelham-Holles, the Duke of Newcastle. Under this coalition of personalities, as opposed to parties, Pitt formulated strategic policy, appointed commanders, and provided vision and energy, without actually holding the title of First Lord of the Treasury or Prime Minister. Some designate Pitt as the true 'Prime Minister' for this period, though most sources list Newcastle, who secured the backing of Parliament and provided George II with a premier the king could personally tolerate (he detested Pitt).

Pitt's brilliantly successful prosecution of the Seven Years' War was due in large part to his determination to control the oceans through the strength of the Royal Navy. While French armies were being neutralised on the European continent and stranded in isolated colonial Canadian forts, Britain was able to reinforce and supply her far-flung armies around the world due to her naval supremacy. Pitt's diplomatic faith in, and financial support of, Prussia under Frederick the Great provided continuous military pressure against France on the European continent. His keen promotion of commanding officers of talent and imagination, over those of greater seniority but lesser ability, further demonstrated his determined pursuit of success.

By 1761 victory was virtually assured, but the costs of this epic struggle – one that many have since labelled the first 'world' war – continued to spiral ever upward. Britain's new king, George III, spurred the growing disenchantment over taxes to fund the war, and Pitt's desire to further expand the war by attacking Spain led to dwindling support in Parliament and the resignation of Newcastle. Both George III and his new Prime Minister, the Earl of Bute, sought peace. The ensuing Treaty of Paris (1763) ended the Seven Years' War but was heavily criticised by Pitt, setting the stage for his own resignation. By now Pitt's health, both mental and physical, was under severe strain and he retreated to his estate at Hayes where he sought the comfort and support of his wife and family.

Pitt had married in 1754 Hester Grenville, sister of future Prime Minster George Grenville. One of their four children, William Pitt (the Younger), was to become a formidable Prime Minister in his own right, waging a lengthy crusade against Napoleonic France. Pitt (the Elder) dealt with his physical and mental demons by enjoying periods of rest and comfort at his estate, interspersed with energetic bouts of politics. In particular, he took the question of governing the North American colonies as high cause for patience and care. Pitt considered these colonists to be fellow English citizens with all of the 'Rights of Englishmen', and the thirteen American colonies to be the crown jewels of Britain's economic empire. He fought vigorously for repeal of the divisive Stamp Act and opposed severe punishment for those in North America who rejected the unpopular taxes. His efforts were in vain, as the cycle of events that would lead to the American Revolutionary War was already beginning to spin out of control.

Pitt returned to power as the recognised Prime Minister in 1766, the same year that he took a title, Earl of Chatham, and left the House of Commons. Pitt attempted to offer sympathy and restraint in dealings with the North American colonies in order to retain them within the British Empire, but this proved futile. In the North American wilderness, the former French Fort Duquesne, on the Ohio River, was renamed Fort Pitt in his honour – today it is Pittsburgh, Pennsylvania.

Pitt's health was steadily deteriorating and he was forced to resign in 1768. He continually voiced his concern over the American colonies but to no avail. Even during the Revolutionary War, Pitt was still seeking to retain the colonies as loyal and friendly members of the British Empire. His last major political act was in opposition to proposals for the independence of the colonies, hoping to keep them loyal and favoured. But it was all for naught.

Shortly thereafter, in April 1778, Pitt collapsed and died. He is buried in Westminster Abbey. His contributions to British and world history cannot be overestimated, and to many historians he is no less than the founder of Britain's world empire.

George III
(reigned 1760–1820).

AUGUSTUS HENRY FITZROY

DUKE OF GRAFTON

Born: 28 September 1735
Died: 14 March 1811
Party: Whig
Served: 14 October 1768 – 28 January 1770
(1 year, 106 days)

*"Wisdom is at no time more
conspicuous, nor more amiable,
than in the acknowledgement
of error"*

AUGUSTUS HENRY FITZROY, the 3rd Duke of Grafton, was Prime Minister under King George III from 1767 to 1770. Fitzroy was a direct descendant (fourth generation) of the illegitimate son of Charles II and one of his mistresses, Barbara Villiers. Both he and modern-day Prime Minister David Cameron can claim a direct connection to the Crown, even if only through an illegitimate affair.

Fitzroy was born in 1735, the grandson of the 2nd Duke of Grafton, and the son of Lord Augustus Fitzroy and Elizabeth Cosby. He was educated at Cambridge and served briefly in the House of Commons at the age of twenty-one, before assuming the title of Duke upon the death of his grandfather, his father having already died.

Grafton was an admirer of William Pitt, and was among those young Whig politicians who were cast out of office by Prime Minister John Stuart (Earl of Bute) after the fall of the Duke of Newcastle's government. Having lost his position as Lord Lieutenant of Suffolk, Grafton and the other dismissed Whigs determined to undermine Bute and his anti-Pitt policies. In the meantime, Grafton devoted much time, energy, and money to his other passions: breeding racehorses, collecting books, and enjoying women (it seems he was cut from the same cloth as his ancestor, Charles II).

Grafton had five children, three of whom survived infancy, with his first wife Anne Liddell, while conducting a socially open and scandalous relationship with Nancy Anne Parsons – a woman known as Mrs Houghton, who had an already vivid history of affairs. Eventually, his wife ran off with the Earl of Upper Ossory, a racy scandal in itself, but convenient, since it allowed Grafton to divorce Liddell and marry Elizabeth

Wrottesley, with whom he had thirteen children. He was rumoured to have fathered over a dozen additional illegitimate children.

Politically, Grafton was completely wedded to William Pitt. Weakening support for the Earl of Bute's Tory government brought a return to Whig power. When Charles Watson-Wentworth, Marquess of Rockingham, became Prime Minister, Grafton took the post of Secretary of State for the Northern Department, with the belief that William Pitt would be included in the government. When Pitt was excluded, Grafton resigned. Rockingham, too, suffered from lack of support, and it was not long before William Pitt, now Earl of Chatham, was asked to form a government. Deteriorating health led Pitt to appoint Grafton as First Lord of the Treasury, though it was Pitt who was actually directing government affairs. Pitt's failing health forced Grafton to take on more and more governmental responsibilities, hence the frequent confusion in the dates of Pitt and Grafton's premierships. By 1768 Grafton was completely, but reluctantly, in charge.

Meanwhile, the John Wilkes affair impacted upon parliamentary politics. Wilkes' crusade for parliamentary reform, coupled with his blistering attacks on the King, led to his eventual arrest, conviction, and imprisonment. Nonetheless, Wilkes was repeatedly re-elected to his Middlesex seat in Parliament, and what to do about Wilkes and his followers plagued several administrations. More vexing, however, was the problem of the defiant American colonies.

Grafton could not prevent parliamentary leader Charles Townshend from pushing through a string of new taxes on the American colonies to replace the repealed Stamp Act. This resulted in a new outburst of colonial protests, boycotts, and violence, culminating in the Boston Massacre of 1770. The Townshend tax duties were subsequently repealed with the exception of the tax on tea. That of course led to the famous Boston Tea Party and the increasing rupture between the colonies and the mother country.

Grafton was neither qualified nor experienced enough to manage these problems – problems that would have challenged the most imaginative leader. The argument over how to deal with the question of the American colonies was running headlong out of control and would soon lead to rebellion and war. Reeling under scathing attacks in the press and lacking any true direction in policy, Grafton resigned in early 1770.

Grafton's only future role in government was as Lord Privy Seal under Prime Ministers Lord North (1771–75) and the Earl of Shelburne (1782). Following in Pitt's footsteps, he recommended moderation in policy toward the American colonies.

Grafton retired to his estate in Suffolk, served as Chancellor of Cambridge University, and wrote several religious essays. His stable of horses was successful in winning the Derby three times. He died on 14 March 1811 and is buried at St Genevieve church, on the grounds of his Suffolk estate, Euston Hall.

FREDERICK NORTH

LORD NORTH

Born: 13 April 1732
Died: 5 August 1792
Party: Tory
Served: 28 January 1770 – 22 March 1782
(12 years, 58 days)

"Men may be popular without being ambitious. But there is hardly an ambitious man who does not try to be popular"

FREDERICK NORTH served as Prime Minister under King George III from 1770 to 1782. And it is North who is commonly saddled with the blame and responsibility for the loss of the American colonies during the American Revolutionary War, which proved to be Britain's first substantial diplomatic and military failure during the eighteenth century.

North was born in 1732, the son of Francis North, 1st Earl of Guildford, and Lady Lucy Montague. Upon leaving Oxford in 1754, North entered Parliament for Banbury, a seat he held for the next thirty-six years. North married Anne Speke in 1736; they had several children, but were supported by very little income. North's reliance on George III extended from political positions to financial backing. He enjoyed this backing until near the end of his premiership when the King lost faith in him over war policy in the American colonies. The King wished to pursue the war, while North felt the cause was now lost and the effort useless.

Initially, North was a follower of the Whig grandees, owing allegiance to William Pitt, Charles Townshend, and the Duke of Newcastle. This relationship, along with his intelligence and popularity in the House of Commons, gave North his rapid rise in government. His support for the expulsion of John Wilkes from the Commons, and the maintenance of the tea tax on the American colonies, endeared him to the King and signalled a shift to a more Tory position. By 1771, North felt that the crisis with the American colonies had been tempered, if not settled. With increased opposition from North's former Whig allies concerning the colonial issues, and with the Duke of Grafton's resignation, the King felt he had a trusted replacement in Lord North as Prime Minister.

In New England in December 1773, after radicals boarded merchant ships and dumped taxed tea into Boston Harbor (the Boston Tea Party), the decision was made to send more British troops to Boston and to close the harbour. Far from quelling matters, it served only to further alienate the already disgruntled New England colonies, and worse, generated sympathy and support from most of the other North American colonies. By 1775, the situation had grown entirely out of hand, with open conflict breaking out throughout New England. By July 1776, a state of war existed between the American colonies and their mother country, with neither side either able or willing to back down.

The strategic defeat of British forces at Saratoga, New York in the autumn of 1777 brought the French into the war on the side of the colonists. After the debacle at Saratoga, North claimed he was not a fit wartime leader and offered George III his resignation, but it was refused. Britain's numerous battlefield victories and control of colonial cities, coupled with seemingly enormous economic and military advantages, failed to defeat the colonists and extinguish their quest for independence. The British defeat at Yorktown, Virginia in 1781 by a combined American and French army and navy convinced North that further struggle was utterly futile. Peace negotiations commenced, and though George III refused to accept the idea that the war could not be won, he did accept North's resignation in 1782. The independence of the thirteen rebellious colonies was formally acknowledged in the Treaty of Paris in 1783.

Lord North was opposed to the treaty, but his lack of power in Parliament, along with his reduced standing in the eyes of the King, eliminated whatever influence he once held. That influence now belonged to the young rising star of the Tory Party, the Younger William Pitt. Now powerless in Parliament and with the King bitter about his failures, North was relegated to a minor role in government.

In 1790, North succeeded his father as 2nd Earl of Guildford, but he lived only two more years, dying in 1792. He is buried in All Saints church, Wroxton, Oxfordshire.

'The State Tinkers' (1780). Lord North (on his knees) and his allies are caricatured by James Gillray as incompetent tinkers of the 'National Kettle'. George III (on the right) is crying out in despair.

WILLIAM PETTY

EARL OF SHELBURNE

Born:	2 May 1737
Died:	7 May 1805
Party:	Whig
Served:	4 July 1782 – 2 April 1783
	(266 days)

"The sun of Great Britain will set whenever she acknowledges the independence of America [which] would end in the ruin of England"

WILLIAM PETTY was Prime Minister under King George III from July 1782 until April 1783. Although Prime Minister for less than a year, his term of office saw the negotiation of the Treaty of Paris that ended the American War of Independence and formally severed ties between Britain and her thirteen rebellious colonies.

Petty was originally born William Fitzmaurice, the son of John and Mary Fitzmaurice. The name Petty was taken when his father, the 1st Earl Shelburne, inherited the estates of his mother's family. Born in Dublin, young William Petty was raised in Ireland before being sent to Oxford for his education. Petty's early career was in the military, serving in the Seven Years' War as a colonel of the Foot Guards and later as an aide-de-camp to George III. In 1761, upon his father's death, Petty became the 2nd Earl of Shelburne and entered the House of Lords. He assumed several ministerial posts: First Lord of Trade under George Grenville, Secretary of State under William Pitt the Elder, and Home Secretary under Charles Watson-Wentworth (Marquess of Rockingham). He was occupying the latter position when Rockingham died in July 1782, enabling Petty to become First Lord of the Treasury and Prime Minister.

As Prime Minister, Shelburne's months in office were a struggle from the beginning. His family was new to wealth and title, and though a Whig, he was never accepted by the Whig Party grandees. These grandees were from families who not only enjoyed great wealth and privilege, but who also descended from long lines of entitled nobility. Shelburne was always considered an outsider, lacking the approved pedigree and social graces.

Though a loyal Whig, Shelburne tended to feel a greater obligation to his nation than to his party. This political philosophy did not win him many admirers. His devotion to

William Pitt the Elder, his sympathy for James Wilkes – the accused libeller of the King – and his belief that the American colonies should be treated with greater respect and equality in order to preserve their loyalty, these all ran against the popular political grain. As Prime Minister, Shelburne lacked support in the House of Commons and was bitterly opposed by fellow Whig minister James Fox, who was in turn despised and distrusted by George III. Shelburne lacked allies on all fronts, and his administration and reputation were virtually doomed from the start.

Shelburne's brief premiership became dominated by the question of how to end the war with the American colonies. Shelburne and Fox had both participated in the peace negotiations under the Rockingham regime. When Rockingham died and Shelburne became Prime Minister, Fox sought to dismantle and defeat any treaty engineered by Shelburne, even if the treaty terms were amenable to the Whig majority. Shelburne concluded the Treaty of Paris and presented it to a hostile Parliament. The war would end, the thirteen colonies would be granted independence, British loyalists in America would be promised fair treatment and compensated for loss, and numerous territories around the world would be exchanged between England, France, Spain, and Holland. Fox and the Whigs in Parliament saw to it that the treaty was twice defeated, forcing Shelburne's resignation in February 1783. William Cavendish-Bentinck (Duke of Portland) became Prime Minister and within six months a virtually identical treaty was passed and accepted by a reluctant King and Parliament, who blamed Shelburne for failure to secure better terms. In reality, Britain was sick of the war, anxious to get out of it, and generally willing to now bid good riddance to the colonies and their expensive war of rebellion. Shelburne became the scapegoat and never held political office again.

Shelburne was married to Lady Sophie Carteret, the daughter of the 1st Earl Granville. They had two sons before she died at the early age of twenty-five. He later married Lady Louise Fitzpatrick, the daughter of the 1st Earl of Upper Ossory, producing another son and daughter. During his brief premiership, Shelburne had recognised the budding brilliance of William Pitt the Younger and promoted him to Chancellor of the Exchequer at the age of only twenty-three. Later, as Prime Minister, the Younger Pitt raised Shelburne to the title of Marquess of Landsdowne.

Much of Shelburne/Landsdowne's later life was spent at his quintessentially English country estate of Bowood, where he championed and encouraged scientists and intellectuals such as Joseph Priestley and Jeremy Bentham. He was derisively nicknamed 'Malagrida', or the Jesuit of Berkeley Square, for his reputation as being devious and insincere. He died in 1805 and is buried in High Wycombe church, Buckinghamshire. Even in death and burial he could not escape his ignominious reputation for failure and the blame for the loss of the American colonies. His name is not commemorated on any burial wall or floor plaque, supposedly because of his disgrace in connection with the negotiation and settlement of the Treaty of Paris. There is a lone, almost obscure reference to William Petty on a larger Petty monument placed in the church by later generations. Otherwise his burial location is completely ignored.

WILLIAM CAVENDISH-BENTINCK

DUKE OF PORTLAND

Born:	14 April 1738
Died:	30 October 1809
Party:	Whig/Tory
Served:	2 April 1783 –19 December 1783
	31 March 1807 – 4 October 1809
	(3 years, 82 days)

*"My fears are not that the attempt
to perform will shorten my life,
but that I shall neither bodily or
mentally perform as I should"
(on becoming PM again late in life)*

WILLIAM CAVENDISH-BENTINCK was twice Prime Minister under King George III. As the 3rd Duke of Portland, he was born to great wealth and position, another of the Whig grandees who figure prominently in much of eighteenth and early nineteenth-century politics. Both of his terms of office were predicated on a need to find common ground within a divided Whig Party. His interests lay more in bridging divergent party wings than in being a leader to point in new directions or inspire action. Portland distinguished himself for nearly a half century as a skilful Whig politician and holder of high office, and the fact that he is not considered a great or formidable Prime Minister should not detract from his faithful and diligent service within Parliament. He never sought the premiership through any burning ambition, but instead undertook the office out of a sense of duty to king and country. He soldiered on as best he could in the circumstances he encountered, entirely understanding his own lack of initiative or desire to be a decisive influence upon the events that swirled around him.

He was born in 1738, the son of William Bentinck, 2nd Duke of Portland, and Lady Margaret Harley. He was educated at Eton and Oxford, was serving in the House of Commons by the age of twenty-three, and became the 3rd Duke on the death of his father in 1762. Adding more confusion to our modern recognition of eighteenth-century politicians, in 1766 Portland assumed the name Cavendish-Bentinck when he married Lady Dorothy Cavendish, daughter of former Prime Minister William Cavendish, Duke of Devonshire.

Portland served in several governments, frequently holding high office. Upon the death of the Prime Minister Charles Watson-Wentworth (Marquess of Rockingham) in 1782, Bentinck acquired the leadership of Rockingham's wing of the Whig Party. When the Earl of Shelburne was unable to either conclude a treaty of peace with the American colonies or to maintain a viable government, Portland was thrust into the role of Prime Minister. He was no more capable of bringing order to the chaos surrounding him than his predecessor had been. Disagreement over the control of the East India Company, the controversial but eventual signing of the Treaty of Paris granting independence to the thirteen American colonies, and how to pay off the Prince of Wales' enormous debts, all demanded vision and talent beyond Portland's capacity to provide it. George III therefore dismissed him in December of 1783.

He remained head of the Whig Party, although Whig luminaries Charles Fox and Edmund Burke became the leading figures in opposition to the next government. William Pitt the Younger now became Tory Prime Minister, and with the shocking violence of the French Revolution and the ensuing rise of Napoleon Bonaparte, Portland began to gradually edge closer to a Tory point of view. Pitt eventually brought him into his government. When Pitt died in 1806, Portland temporarily retired from politics. This was not to last. By 1807 the William Grenville government had collapsed under seemingly insurmountable problems, not the least of which was Napoleon's apparently unstoppable conquests in Europe. In desperation, King George again called upon Portland to stitch together a government, this time Tory, and bring some stability to the situation. Portland accepted out of a sense of duty, although by now he was elderly and weak with illness. But he did have some assets within his Cabinet. George Canning, Spencer Perceval, Robert Jenkinson (all future Prime Ministers) and Lord Castlereagh provided Portland with capable personnel to effectively confront the considerable challenges that Britain faced. But it wasn't to be. Little was accomplished due to lack of support in the Commons and endless Cabinet rivalry and backbiting, culminating in an infamous duel between Canning and Castlereagh. Portland, now quite ill, resigned in September of 1809 and died in October.

Portland was buried in the crypt of the old parish church of St Marylebone, London (across the street from Madame Tussaud's), a church to which he had liberally donated. Unfortunately for poor William Cavendish-Bentinck, the crypt was completely emptied in 1981 and his remains, along with many others, were quietly moved and re-interred in a mass grave at Brookwood Cemetery in Surrey. There is no formal plaque identifying Bentinck or any of the others, merely a tall white cross with the year of the removal from St Marylebone – a curious and undistinguished final resting place for a two-time British Prime Minister.

WILLIAM PITT THE YOUNGER

Born:	28 May 1759
Died:	23 January 1806
Party:	Tory
Served:	19 December 1783 – 14 March 1801
	10 May 1804 – 23 January 1806
	(18 years, 343 days)

> *"Necessity is the plea for every infringement of human freedom. It is the argument of tyrants; it is the creed of slaves"*

WILLIAM PITT THE YOUNGER was the second son of former Prime Minister William Pitt the Elder, Earl of Chatham, and his wife Hester Grenville. Pitt the Younger served twice as Prime Minister under King George III, 1783–1801 and 1804–06. He was raised on politics and became PM at the tender age of twenty-four. As premier, he devoted considerable time, energy, and determination to the defeat of Napoleon in the interminable Napoleonic Wars. Though unsuccessful in this aim during his lifetime, dying as he did in office at the age of forty-three, his resolve and unrelenting fortitude inspired Britain to persevere in the face of all odds and eventually overcome her continental nemesis.

Pitt was born in 1759, educated at Cambridge, and elected to the House of Commons in 1781. He served as Chancellor of the Exchequer and Leader of the Commons under William Petty (Earl of Shelburne) while only twenty-three years old. The Whig government of Shelburne soon collapsed over the issue of American independence, forcing the resignation of both Shelburne and Pitt. Following a short-lived coalition administration under the Duke of Portland, Pitt took the helm of a Tory Party government that was agreeable to George III. This administration would last for the next eighteen years.

Early in his career, the young Pitt was a firm champion of parliamentary reform and the abolition of slavery. The reform of Parliament would remain unfulfilled for several decades, but on the issue of slavery, Pitt joined forces with the famous anti-slavery reformer William Wilberforce, paving the way for its abolition. Reduction of the debt incurred by the American Revolutionary War became a priority, along with the control of the far-flung British colonies that now stretched around the world from India to Canada. His relationships with the House of Commons and with George III were on solid footing, although the King's bouts of mental illness brought Pitt into conflict with the Prince of Wales. The Prince favoured the Whigs and wished to be declared Regent on account of his father's mental illness, but George III regained his health and Pitt remained in power.

In the 1790s the growing threat of revolutionary France began drawing Britain into numerous European coalitions to stem the tide of French radicalism. For a while, Britain would serve as the last and only impediment to Napoleon's continental supremacy. These wartime coalitions required huge outlays of British treasure to support and defend those European nations willing to continue the struggle of defeating Napoleon. By 1797, the Bank of England was in desperate financial straits, and without Horatio Nelson's great naval victories at the battles of the Nile and Trafalgar in 1798 and 1805 respectively, the country's resolve might have collapsed.

Pitt had also lost the confidence of George III over the question of Irish emancipation, which led to Pitt's resignation in 1802. His successor, albeit briefly, was a fellow Tory, Henry Addington. Pitt became disenchanted with Addington, and his support of the new administration soon faded. By 1804 Pitt had regained the role of Prime Minister, but by then both his political and physical strength were substantially weaker.

Pitt's health had deteriorated to an alarming degree. Though only in his early forties, he had been working himself nearly to death. Defeat of Pitt's third European coalition only seemed to underscore the seeming invincibility of Napoleon. On a doctor's recommendation when he was young man, Pitt had taken to drinking at least a bottle of port a day, and by now his large and continuous consumption of alcohol had begun to take a severe toll on his health.

Pitt the Younger and his nemesis Napoleon are depicted carving up the globe in a contemporary cartoon.

Nelson's great victory at Trafalgar in October 1805 had saved Britain from invasion, but at the tragic cost of Nelson's death. Despite Pitt's endless optimism for eventual success against Bonaparte, in 1806 the Napoleonic Wars were a rather uncertain and unpromising enterprise from a British perspective. Enormously expensive and strategically intractable, the situation for Pitt and his administration had reached perhaps its lowest point. So too had Pitt's health and he died in 1806 at the age of just forty-six, having served nearly nineteen of the last twenty-three years as Prime Minister.

Although there were several suggestions and opportunities for marriage, Pitt remained a bachelor all of his life. Deeply in debt at the time of his death, he was renowned for never having enriched himself at the expense of the nation's treasury, earning him the title of 'Incorruptible'. His debts were repaid by the nation and his goal of defeating Napoleonic France would eventually be accomplished, but not before another nine years of conflict had come to pass.

William Pitt the Younger is buried near his father's final resting place in Westminster Abbey.

'A Voluptuary under the Horrors of Digestion'. James Gillray's caricature of 1792 depicts the Prince of Wales, the future Prince Regent and George IV (reigned 1820–30), in a very unflattering light. Pitt the Younger and the Prince did not see eye to eye.

HENRY ADDINGTON

LORD SIDMOUTH

Born:	30 May 1757
Died:	15 February 1844
Party:	Tory
Served:	17 March 1801 – 10 May 1804
	(3 years, 54 days)

"In youth, the absence of pleasure is pain; in old age the absence of pain is pleasure"

HENRY ADDINGTON was Prime Minister under King George III, splitting Pitt the Younger's two terms in office. He was the son of a physician, Dr Anthony Addington, and Mary Hiley. Dr Addington had treated Pitt the Elder for his bouts of mental illness. This brought Henry into contact with the powerful Pitt family, and he became close friends with Pitt the Younger, thereby establishing their political alliance.

Addington is the first Prime Minister not to emerge from the landed gentry. His family background was deemed 'professional', a fact that led to much ridicule of Addington and his policies. Educated at Oxford and trained for the law, he was habitually referred to as 'The Doctor', which in referring to his father's occupation was intended to highlight his lack of a title and his supposedly inferior social status.

With Pitt's support, Addington gained political prominence and entered Parliament in 1784, becoming Speaker of the House of Commons in 1789. Pitt valued Addington's intelligence and calm manner, but most importantly, his grasp of financial matters. When Pitt's first premiership foundered on the question of Catholic emancipation, Pitt offered his resignation and recommended Addington as his replacement. George III assented to both requests and Addington became PM.

From the outset, Addington lacked party support in Parliament; he had no following in the Tory Party and was bereft of family ties to the hereditary grandees and their network of political and social influence. Furthermore, he faced the continuing challenge of Napoleonic warfare and diplomacy, which had so plagued his predecessor. Addington was successful, however, in paying off much of the enormous debt incurred by Pitt's government in fighting Napoleonic France. His acceptance of the Treaty of

Amiens ushered in a period of peace for Britain to catch her breath, placing the nation on a firmer financial footing and better positioned for the inevitable future wars with Napoleon, which were soon to come.

For his efforts, Addington was accused of giving away too much in the Treaty of Amiens, allowing war to break out again with France, and then doing a poor job of waging the renewed war against Napoleon. Condemnation of Addington's war management came from all sides and all political parties; even his former champion, Pitt, joined in the chorus of criticism. With no support either in or out of Parliament, Addington resigned in April 1804. Pitt returned as Prime Minister and Addington, though bitter at his treatment, returned to support and participate in Pitt's administration.

Created 1st Viscount Sidmouth in 1805, Addington shuttled in and out of numerous government positions in a variety of later administrations, retiring from his Cabinet posts in 1827. He had married Ursula Hammond in 1791, but after her death in 1823 he married Mary Anne Stowell. His first marriage produced two sons and four daughters.

As Home Secretary from 1812 to 1822, Addington was witness to the bitter confrontation between post-war anti-industrial opponents, such as the factory-destroying Luddites, and the irresistible forces of progressive industrialization. Many of his responses were deemed harsh and cruel, though the methods used by the anti-industrial mobs were anything but gentle. Addington's belief in the inevitability of progress and modern industry won out in the end.

In retrospect, though not generally rated in the top rank of British Prime Ministers, Addington certainly took more initial criticism than seems justified. Much of the abuse stemmed from his perceived lack of family pedigree, and even his elevation to the peerage was scorned by many as a dilution of the titled ranks. But his reordering of Britain's finances in preparation for Pitt's third coalition against Napoleon showed that he was capable of major positive accomplishments. He was most assuredly not liberal in his politics, remaining opposed to Catholic emancipation as late as 1829 and voting against the Reform Bill of 1832, but he was at least consistent in these policies and certainly not alone in his obstinacy. Along with men such as George Canning, Addington paved the way for non-titled professionals and commoners to rise to the highest levels of government.

Henry Addington died in 1844. He is buried in the cemetery of St Mary Magdalene's church, Mortlake, London.

WILLIAM GRENVILLE

BARON GRENVILLE

Born:	24 October 1759
Died:	12 January 1834
Party:	Whig
Served:	11 February 1806 – 31 March 1807
	(1 year, 42 days)

"I can hardly keep wondering at my own folly in thinking it worthwhile to leave my books and garden, even for one day's attendance in the House of Commons"

WILLIAM GRENVILLE served as Prime Minister under King George III. Grenville came from a well-connected family; his father, George Grenville, had also served as Prime Minister under George III, from 1763 to 1765. His mother, Elizabeth Wyndham, was the daughter of Sir William Wyndham and granddaughter of the Duke of Somerset.

Educated at Eton and Oxford, William Grenville entered Parliament in 1782. He was a cousin of Pitt the Younger, who quickly promoted him to Paymaster-General, then Speaker of the House of Commons, and by 1789, Home Secretary. In 1790, Pitt ennobled Grenville as Baron Grenville and installed him as Leader of the House of Lords. In 1791, Grenville married Pitt's cousin, Anne Pitt, daughter of Lord Camelford. They had no children.

As Pitt's Foreign Secretary (1791–1801), it became Grenville's mission to confront the crisis surrounding revolutionary France and the subsequent rise of Napoleon. Pitt embarked upon a succession of coalitions with like-minded European nations to militarily challenge Napoleon's aggressive domination of Europe. Following Pitt's resignation in 1801, fellow Tory Henry Addington became Prime Minister. Unhappy with Addington's performance, Grenville adopted a strong voice of opposition and gradually shifted his support to the Whigs.

By 1804, Addington's failures had brought Pitt back into power. New coalitions brought some success, notably Nelson's great victory at Trafalgar in October 1805, but Napoleon remained nearly invincible on land, especially after his decisive victory at Austerlitz in December 1805. The strain on Pitt, his Tory government, and the nation as a whole was enormous. When Pitt, only forty-six years old, died in 1806, Grenville became Prime Minister.

Grenville and his government attempted to make peace with Napoleon while continuing to fight an expensive and increasingly global war. Neither tactic was particularly successful. Grenville sought a wide-based administration, the so-called 'Ministry of All the Talents', in an effort to bring about domestic reforms. Abolition of the slave trade was accomplished, but a renewed attempt to further the cause of Catholic emancipation failed and brought down Grenville's government in 1807.

During the next decade of Tory governments, Grenville led the Whig opposition. The Napoleonic Wars finally came to an end with the defeat of Napoleon at Waterloo in 1815. As post-war social disturbances in Britain increased in intensity, Grenville shifted his support back to the Tory Party and Prime Minister Lord Liverpool's government. By 1817, Grenville had abandoned his leadership of the Whig opposition and by 1821 was fully supporting Liverpool (though refusing office). Retiring from politics and government after suffering a stroke in 1823, he continued as Chancellor of the University of Oxford (a role he had undertaken since 1810) until his death in 1834. Except for the Pitts, George and William Grenville remain the only father and son to both serve as Prime Minister. William Grenville is buried in St Peter's church, Burnham, Buckinghamshire, near what was once his large estate at Dropmore Lodge.

Napoleon in his imperial robes, as painted by Jean Auguste Dominique Ingres in 1806. The French emperor proved a constant cause of concern for British Prime Ministers of this period.

SPENCER PERCEVAL

Born: 1 November 1762
Died: 11 May 1812
Party: Tory
Served: 4 October 1809 – 11 May 1812
           (2 years, 221 days)

> *"I have nothing more to say to*
> *the nothing that has been said"*
> *(during a debate)*

SPENCER PERCEVAL was Prime Minister under King George III. He is the only British Prime Minister to have been assassinated, being shot and killed in the lobby of the House of Commons on 11 May 1812 by a deranged gunman who held a grievance against the government. His death came at a time when Britain and her coalition of European nations were finally approaching success in the interminable war with Napoleon Bonaparte. Britain had endured extended internal turmoil and expended vast amounts of treasure and political capital in attempting to bring down Napoleon and his European empire. Several Prime Ministers had agonised over the course of action and degree of effort. Spencer Perceval maintained William Pitt's determination to defeat Napoleon but, like Pitt, would not live to savour that victory.

Perceval was the second son of John Perceval, Earl of Egmont, and his second wife, Catherine Compton. Educated at Cambridge, Perceval studied law and entered the House of Commons in 1796. He was a devoted follower of Pitt the Younger and was as dedicated to the defeat of Napoleon as his patron. Perceval, however, did have his own views; he opposed Pitt's plan for Catholic emancipation and later opposed Grenville and the Whigs' efforts to abolish the slave trade. But his bedrock Tory position – the continuation of the struggle to rid Europe of Napoleonic domination – remained steadfast.

When William Cavendish-Bentinck (Duke of Portland) resigned in 1809 due to ill health, Perceval was not the obvious choice to become PM. Both George Canning and Robert Stewart (Lord Castlereagh) were highly qualified and had strong Tory support. But their endless feuding with each other negated their considerable strengths. Perceval was respected for his integrity and quiet determination, qualities that served him well in the ongoing struggle to maintain a maximum war effort against Napoleon. And this effort was beginning to show signs of bearing fruit. While Wellington's army was demonstrating great success on the Iberian Peninsula, Russia was openly challenging Napoleon's continental economic policy, and Britain's Royal Navy still dominated the seas. Nearly two decades of struggle were finally paying off.

Unfortunately, fate denied Perceval the pleasure of experiencing victory, his life being cut short by his assassination. The assassin, John Bellingham, was a merchant who felt that the government had wronged him and therefore owed him compensation. In a deranged act of irrationality, Bellingham appeared at the House of Commons and shot and killed Perceval. Giving himself up immediately, Bellingham was arrested, tried and convicted at the Old Bailey in May of 1812. He was executed at Newgate Prison two days later.

Perceval had married Jane Wilson in 1790, and they had twelve children. Since Perceval was not a man of great wealth, his wife and large family were financially compensated after his death by a sympathetic Parliament. A dedicated evangelical in his religious practice and philosophy, he is buried in the crypt of St Luke's church, Charlton, London.

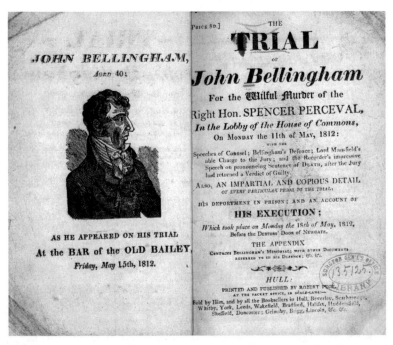

A contemporary pamphlet detailing for popular consumption the trial and execution of Perceval's murderer, John Bellingham.

ROBERT JENKINSON

EARL OF LIVERPOOL

Born:	7 June 1770
Died:	4 December 1828
Party:	Tory
Served:	8 June 1812 – 9 April 1827
	(14 years, 305 days)

"[I consider] the right of election as a public trust, granted not for the benefit of the individual, but for the public good"

ROBERT JENKINSON, Earl of Liverpool, served as Prime Minister under Georges III and IV. It was Liverpool who oversaw the final defeat of Napoleon Bonaparte and the successful conclusion of the lengthy Napoleonic Wars.

Jenkinson was born in 1770, the eldest son of Charles Jenkinson, later to become the 1st Earl Liverpool, and Amelia Watts. Following an education at Oxford, Jenkinson toured Europe and witnessed the onset of the French Revolution. This experience left him with a lasting impression of the dangers of social and political revolution, no matter how worthy and lofty the original intentions. In 1803, Jenkinson became Lord Hawkesbury when his father received the title of Earl of Liverpool. He entered Parliament in 1790, becoming a loyal follower of Pitt the Younger and his Tory government. In 1795 he married Theodosia Louisa Hervey, daughter of the Earl of Bristol. In 1822, upon the death of his first wife, he married Mary Chester. There were no children from either marriage.

Jenkinson moved quickly up the political ladder, becoming Foreign Secretary in Henry Addington's government and Home Secretary during Pitt's second term as PM. He became the 2nd Earl of Liverpool upon the death of his father in 1808. As leader of the opposition to William Grenville's administration, Liverpool joined with Pitt's friends after the death of Pitt in 1806 to serve in the Tory governments of the Duke of Portland and Spencer Perceval. He became Secretary of State for War and the Colonies under Perceval, in which post he was instrumental in the backing of Wellington's highly successful Spanish campaign against Napoleon. Liverpool's faith in this campaign, coupled with Napoleon's crippling debacle in Russia, led to the coalition victory and first abdication by Napoleon in 1814.

Liverpool became acting Prime Minister after the assassination of Spencer Perceval in 1812, but by the general election later that year, he had fully consolidated his position and would remain PM for the next fifteen years. He wisely declared the issue of Catholic emancipation to be a matter of personal conscience rather than government policy. Neutralising this contentious issue – one that had repeatedly divided previous Tory administrations – allowed Liverpool's government the latitude to deal more effectively with the conclusion of the Napoleonic Wars.

Following his abdication and first exile, Napoleon decided to escape and reclaim power, thus commencing his 'Hundreds Days' of attempting to re-conquer Europe. A desperate panic soon spread across the Continent. Fortunately, both for England and for Europe, the Duke of Wellington and a fresh coalition of English, Dutch and Prussian forces decisively defeated Napoleon at the Battle of Waterloo in 1815. Permanently exiled to the forlorn and isolated Atlantic island of St Helena, Napoleon was now removed from the European political stage once and for all. What could not be erased was the influence of the French and American Revolutions, and Napoleon's very real social and political reforms that would now have an impact on all of future European society.

Jenkinson's government also faced several domestic issues of note. The post-war economic recession, which lasted into the 1820s, spawned outbursts of violence such as the Peterloo Massacre of 1819. Social unrest also surfaced during the suppression of the Luddite movement, as groups of displaced workers naively believed that the destruction of factories and the wrecking of modern machines would preserve traditional jobs requiring manual labour. Of a less violent nature, but no less controversial, was the passage of the Corn Laws, which placed tariffs on imported grain. Liverpool went along with the Corn Laws, even though he personally favoured free trade to invigorate the economy. Britain eventually recovered from her post-war economic doldrums and ultimately prospered, entering a century of spectacular economic growth. This explosion of wealth and economic expansion had no parallel in human history. Indeed, modern technology and advancements could not be denied or contained, and developments accelerated at an astounding pace that seemed threatening to some, frightening to others, and truly astonishing to all.

Two other issues also plagued Parliament and Liverpool's Tory government: the continued question of Catholic emancipation, which would not be solved until the end of the 1820s (splitting another Tory Cabinet in the process), and the divorce of King George IV from his wife Caroline, which ignited a public and political debate that deeply fractured and nearly toppled Liverpool's government.

Though not dramatic or spectacular, Liverpool was respected for his integrity and sound judgement. His management of the final years of the Napoleonic Wars was patient, consistent, and resolute. Yet the new challenges and social dilemmas facing the emerging industrialised world would continue to be confronted well into the future.

Robert Jenkinson, Lord Liverpool, suffered a severe stroke in February 1827 at the age of fifty-seven and duly resigned his post. He died in 1828 and is buried in St Mary's church, Hawkesbury, Gloucestershire.

GEORGE CANNING

Born: 11 April 1770
Died: 8 August 1827
Party: Tory
Served: 10 April 1827 – 8 August 1827
(119 days)

*"Indecision and delays are the
parents of failure"*

GEORGE CANNING became Prime Minister in 1827 under King George IV. He served for less than a year, dying a mere four months into his administration. His personality was a volcanic and flamboyant combination of extremes, though his fundamental political positions ran to moderation. Canning was intelligent and energetic, yet his ability to aggravate his friends and quarrel with his allies often left him unable to achieve his own goals and thwarted the objectives of his party. His bitter enmity towards fellow Cabinet member Robert Stewart (Lord Castlereagh) went far beyond political disagreement, extending to a deep personal ill will. Their quarrel divided the Tory Cabinet and enraged friend and foe alike, eventually leading to an infamous duel on Putney Heath in September 1809. Canning was wounded, injured in the thigh, and both men resigned their Cabinet posts. Of the two, Canning undoubtedly suffered the greater harm to his career.

He was born in 1770, the son of George Canning and Mary Anne Costello. His father died in 1771, leaving his mother to support the family. This she did by becoming an actress and a draper. A prosperous uncle, Stratford Canning, provided the means for his education at Eton and Oxford. Canning did well in school, practised law, and in 1800 married wealthy heiress Joan Scott. In so doing, he obtained financial independence. They had three sons and a daughter.

He entered Parliament in 1793, becoming a dedicated follower of Pitt the Younger, and by 1795 held office in Pitt's administration as Under-Secretary of State for Foreign Affairs. Like Robert Jenkinson (Lord Liverpool), Canning had flirted with the more reform-minded Whig ideas, but the violence of the French Revolution and the threat of the Napoleonic Empire convinced him to solidly support Pitt and the firm Tory commitment to Napoleon's defeat.

Canning was in and out of numerous administrations, and though respected for his brilliance and competence, especially in foreign affairs, he frequently irritated those closest to him with his divisive manner – the Castlereagh affair being the most notorious example. Canning failed on several occasions to attract a large enough following to gain the office of Prime Minister, and due to his still ongoing quarrel with Castlereagh, he missed out on the opportunity during Lord Liverpool's premiership to participate in the peace negotiations following the defeat of Napoleon. Canning eventually returned to government in 1822 as a highly praised Foreign Secretary, replacing his long-time nemesis Lord Castlereagh, who had committed suicide.

It was therefore ironic that, upon finally becoming Prime Minister in 1827, he would suddenly take ill and die within months of assuming office. His only major parliamentary effort was an unsuccessful attempt to carry on Lord Liverpool's effort to abolish the tariff on grain imports, the Corn Laws.

Already suffering from fatigue and a variety of illnesses, and barely four months into his premiership, Canning became ill after attending the Duke of York's funeral. He died shortly afterwards, in August 1827. Perhaps fittingly, George Canning and his great rival and bitter enemy Lord Castlereagh are both buried in Westminster Abbey.

Westminster Abbey, where George Canning and seven other Prime Ministers are buried, namely Pitt the Elder, Pitt the Younger, Lord Palmerston, William Gladstone, Andrew Bonar Law, Neville Chamberlain and Clement Attlee.

FREDERICK ROBINSON

VISCOUNT GODERICH

Born:	30 October 1782
Died:	28 January 1859
Party:	Tory
Served:	31 August 1827 – 21 January 1828 (130 days)

"There was no one good in this life that had not with it some concomitant evil"

FREDERICK ROBINSON, Viscount Goderich, served as Prime Minister under King George IV, replacing the deceased George Canning whose administration had lasted but four months. Robinson's was to last only five months, cut short by his inability to successfully solve the divisive issues of Catholic emancipation and parliamentary reform. He was not in office long enough to face Parliament, and it is said that King George IV provided a handkerchief upon Robinson's tearful resignation.

Robinson was born in 1782, the second son of Thomas Robinson, Lord Grantham, and Lady Mary Yorke. Educated at Cambridge, he entered Parliament in 1806, served in the administrations of several Tory Prime Ministers, and successfully spent 1812–23 at the Board of Trade as Vice-President and later as President. In 1813, he married the wealthy heiress Lady Sarah Hobart, daughter of the Earl of Buckinghamshire. They had two sons and one daughter.

Economic and financial planning were Robinson's greatest strengths, reflected in his becoming Chancellor of the Exchequer under Robert Jenkinson (Lord Liverpool). When Canning became PM in 1827, Robinson was named Secretary of State for War and the Colonies and was created Viscount Goderich. Canning's sudden death encouraged George IV to ask Goderich to form a government. From the start, Goderich felt out of his depth as a leader. The Catholic emancipation question had divided Tory administrations dating back to Pitt the Younger. Repeal of the Corn Laws (tariffs on imported grain) had plagued Liverpool and Canning, and had long troubled Goderich as being economically irresponsible. And the overall pressure for parliamentary reform, which had been building for a generation, was about to unleash bitter political polarization within government and among society at large. These enormous issues, enough to challenge the strongest of leaders, were overwhelming for a man of Goderich's modest talents and inclinations to even engage, let alone overcome. It remains unclear whether Goderich resigned or was dismissed, but there can be no doubt as to his distress and emotional relief when he left office in January 1828. His replacement, Arthur Wellesley, the Duke of Wellington, did not see fit to find a place for him in the new administration.

Goderich drifted back and forth in his parliamentary positions, supporting both Whig and Tory policies as they presented themselves. He supported Catholic emancipation, the abolition of slavery in the colonies, parliamentary reform, and repeal of the Corn Laws. His efficiency and dependability led to him being selected for several government posts under Whig PM Charles Grey and Tory PM Sir Robert Peel.

Goderich was created Earl of Ripon in 1833, and retired from public office after 1846. His Lincolnshire home in Nocton was his great escape, and like many beleaguered leaders, he took refuge at his country house whenever possible. He died in 1859 at his Putney Heath residence in London and is buried in All Saints church, Nocton, Lincolnshire. He remains one of the most obscure and least written about Prime Ministers in British history.

'The Man That Thought To Stem The Tide'. Goderich's successor, the Duke of Wellington, is depicted in a contemporary cartoon trying the resist the waves of parliamentary reform.

ARTHUR WELLESLEY

DUKE OF WELLINGTON

Born:	*c.* 1 May 1769
Died:	14 September 1852
Party:	Tory
Served:	22 January 1828 – 16 November 1830
	(2 years, 320 days)

"An extraordinary affair. I gave them their orders and they wanted to stay and discuss them" (on his first Cabinet meeting as PM)

ARTHUR WELLESLEY, the Duke of Wellington, was Prime Minister at the end of the reign of George IV and the beginning of the reign of William IV. Wellington's successful career as a military leader during the Napoleonic Wars had brought him enormous fame and fortune. His victories over French forces during the long Peninsula War and his defeat of Napoleon at the Battle of Waterloo would forever place him in the pantheon of the most distinguished British soldiers, ranking alongside Marlborough and Nelson in achievements and honours. His political role, though not on the scale of his military accomplishments, nevertheless brought him to the centre of the two great issues of his time: Catholic emancipation and the Great Reform Bill.

Wellesley was born in Dublin in 1769, the fourth son of Garret Wellesley, 1st Earl of Mornington, and Anne Hill. He began his education at Eton, but could not afford to continue there after the death of his father. Instead, he was commissioned into the army in 1787, starting out as an aide-de-camp, before becoming lieutenant-colonel of his regiment. He saw action in France and India, serving under his brother, the 2nd Earl of Mornington. After his successful military operations in India, Wellesley returned to England, becoming a Member of Parliament in 1806.

In 1808, Wellesley began his famous five-year campaign in Portugal and Spain against the French. His triumphs brought him the titles of Viscount (1809), Marquess (1810), and finally Duke (1814). Following victory at Waterloo in 1815, Wellesley (now the Duke of Wellington) joined Lord Liverpool's Cabinet as Master-General of Ordnance (1819–27). His political contributions steadily increased and reached a turning point over the issue of Catholic emancipation. In protest to this initiative,

Wellington and other Tory leaders who were completely opposed to the policy resigned their offices in George Canning's government.

Canning died after only four months in office, and there followed Frederick Robinson's (Viscount Goderich) further unsuccessful five months. Wellington was then chosen to form a government. Despite his personal opposition to Catholic emancipation, he understood it would be politically necessary and inevitable. In the face of bitter accusations of betrayal from his own party, he reversed his position and ensured the passage through Parliament of the Catholic Relief Act (1829).

Concerning parliamentary reform, Wellington and the Tories remained adamantly opposed to it. Many within his own party were still angry over Wellington's concession on the Catholic issue and withdrew their support, causing his government to collapse in November 1830. When Charles Grey and the Whig Party regained power for the first time in twenty-three years, it was with the express purpose of enacting historic parliamentary reform, which they did, in spite of the strenuous objections of Wellington and his Tory followers. The Great Reform Act of 1832 was the landmark result.

But Wellington did have a hand in other reforms. He had instituted a strengthened police force for the city of Dublin while Chief Secretary for Ireland (1807–09) and became a firm supporter of Robert Peel's introduction of the London Metropolitan Police force (the 'Bobbies') in 1829. Peel introduced the necessary legislation in the Commons and Wellington did so in the Lords. The latter gradually conceded the Tory leadership to the former, though Wellington did continue to serve in several governments as Foreign Secretary (1834–35) and Minister without Portfolio (1841–46) under Peel's premiership. Wellington declined the premiership in 1834, but agreed to serve as caretaker PM while awaiting Peel's return from a trip to Italy. The Duke also resumed the position of Commander-in-Chief of the Army (1842–52).

Wellington had married Catherine Pakenham in 1806, but was never happy with the association. She died in 1831 at the age of fifty-eight. The marriage produced two sons. In his lifetime, Wellington was awarded countless honours, titles, and rewards, including his stately Hyde Park Corner mansion – Apsley House. Then located on the outskirts of London, it today sits squarely in the middle of the capital, is still owned by the Wellington family, and is open to visitors as a museum. The capital city of New Zealand, Wellington, is named after this illustrious soldier and statesman.

Wellington died in September 1852. After a large and elaborate funeral, the 'Iron Duke' was laid to rest in the crypt of St Paul's Cathedral.

CHARLES GREY

EARL GREY

Born:	13 March 1764
Died:	17 July 1845
Party:	Whig
Served:	22 November 1830 – 9 July 1834
	(3 years, 229 days)

"Politics is a pursuit which I detest, which interferes with all my private comfort, and which I only sigh for an opportunity of abandoning for ever."

CHARLES GREY, the 2nd Earl Grey, served as Prime Minister from 1830 to 1834, leading a Whig government under King William IV. It was Grey's championing of the Great Reform Bill of 1832 that helped usher in the sort of parliamentary democratic government that we take for granted today.

Grey was born in 1764 at Falloden, Northumberland, the eldest surviving son of General Charles Grey, later the 1st Earl Grey, and his wife Elizabeth. After education at Eton and Cambridge, Grey began a Grand Tour of Europe, a common venture for those born to wealth and privilege. He also embarked on the twin pursuits of politics and romance. His marriage in 1794 to Mary Elizabeth Ponsonby brought Grey into social and political contact with the liberal establishment of Ireland. It also ended his scandalously open affair with Georgiana Cavendish, the Duchess of Devonshire. From that point on, Grey became a devoted husband and father, relishing the time spent at his Northumberland estate of Howick Hall. This remote and relaxing retreat was a perfect setting for Grey to dote on his fifteen children, ten sons and five daughters, and provided him with lifelong satisfaction.

His early politics centered around parliamentary reform, Catholic emancipation, and engaging with reform-minded personalities such as Charles James Fox. Grey initially supported peace with Napoleonic France in opposition to Pitt the Younger and the Tory commitment to war, but later broke with Fox over the issue. After Pitt's death in 1806, Grey and the Whigs came to power in the government of William Grenville, the so-called 'Ministry of all the Talents', which saw Grey serving as First Lord of the Admiralty and later as Foreign Secretary. When the Tories regained control in 1807, it marked the beginning of Grey and the Whigs' relegation to opposition for the next twenty-three years. Grey literally retreated to his family and estate.

In those twenty-three years, Grey had perhaps several opportunities to form a government, but the time was not auspicious for the reforms that Grey and the Whigs had in mind, namely the reform of parliamentary membership and expanding the franchise. Political momentum would need to be built up. Even then, the Reform Bill of 1832 had to be muscled into law through political coercion and bluff in the face of those who thought it went too far. As moderate as it appears today in hindsight, it was bitterly contested at the time of its passage.

But what was the Reform Bill of 1832? In simple terms it attempted to do two things. Firstly, it would eliminate unfairly or under-represented parliamentary districts. For example, the sparsely populated county of Cornwall sent forty-four MPs to Parliament, while the City of London with a population of over 100,000, sent only four. These under-populated 'rotten boroughs', and the single-landowner districts controlled by aristocratic landowning families known as the 'pocket boroughs', effectively controlled representation in the House of Commons. Secondly, the Reform Bill acknowledged the demand for a greater portion of the population to be enfranchised with the right to vote. This demand was accompanied by the nasty threat of riots and mob violence. Yet the cry was not new. There had been strenuous calls for reform in the mid-eighteenth century, but following the radical violence of the French Revolution, the mood in Parliament was cautious. By 1829, under the premiership of the Duke of Wellington, Catholic emancipation (a generally Whig-supported reform) had been achieved. For the Whigs, this newly expanded voting bloc – coupled with the death of George IV in 1830 and the accession to the throne of his slightly more liberal brother William IV – provided the opening that Grey felt was opportune for passing the Reform Bill. He was proven to be correct.

As Prime Minister, Charles Grey was no flaming radical, but he did have the tenacity and conviction to stand up to the King, to considerable negative aristocratic opinion, and to the stubbornly resistant House of Lords. Success in the House of Commons was not enough. Upon the Lords' rejection of the Reform Bill, Grey demanded of King William the introduction of enough new Lords to overwhelm the votes of the intransigents. Wellington and the Tories had fought long and hard for rejection of the Bill in the House of Lords, but lack of support for his position in the Commons, coupled with the outbreak of several riots across England, forced Wellington to see that the game was up and the Bill eventually became law.

Further progress was made under Grey's leadership following elections to a newly reformed Parliament. In 1833 slavery was abolished in the British Empire, Scottish burghs became open to election, and a degree of child labour protection was achieved in the form of the Factory Act of 1833.

Fractures between radical and conservative factions of the Whig Party led to the unravelling of Grey's ministry. The reform element would eventually evolve into the Liberal Party, while the former Whig Party would gradually wither and disappear. At the age of seventy, Grey resigned the premiership in 1834 and returned to Howick Hall to live out his days on the peaceful Northumberland estate he so deeply cherished.

Before dying in 1845, Grey tended to his large family and estate, and enjoyed his private blend of 'Earl Grey' tea. The story goes that the water on the Howick estate had too much lime in it, ruining the flavour of tea. Grey engaged Chinese experts to add flavouring to cover the mineral taste. 'Earl Grey' tea was born to great success. The Grey family has never asked for nor received financial reward, simply being satisfied with the knowledge that their tea remains highly popular and will forever be associated with the 2nd Earl.

Today, Howick Hall Gardens are open to the public, offering visitors the chance to visit and enjoy a serenely flowered and forested piece of Northumberland countryside. Looking much as it did during the 2nd Earl's life, it is a lovely setting of wooded walks and paths. The estate grounds feature a small parish church that contains the elegant tomb of the Prime Minister who ensured the passage of the Great Reform Bill and forever transformed the British political landscape.

The reformed House of Commons in 1833, following the Great Reform Act of 1832.

WILLIAM LAMB

VISCOUNT MELBOURNE

Born:	15 March 1779
Died:	24 November 1848
Party:	Whig
Served:	16 July 1834 – 14 November 1834,
	18 April 1835 – 30 August 1841
	(6 years, 255 days)

"What I want is men who will support me when I am in the wrong" (to a colleague who said he would support Melbourne when he was in the right)

WILLIAM LAMB, 2nd Viscount Melbourne, was twice Prime Minister, first under King William IV and then Queen Victoria. Lamb was born in 1779, the second son of Peniston Lamb, 1st Viscount Melbourne, and Elizabeth Milbanke, daughter of Sir Ralph Milbanke. Lamb was educated at Eton and Cambridge, going on to become a lawyer. The death of his elder brother led Lamb into politics and left him heir to his father's title, which he inherited in 1829.

Lamb entered Parliament in 1806, drifting in and out of office, first with the Whigs, then becoming Secretary for Ireland in the Tory government of George Canning, and staying on during the Duke of Wellington's administration. Lamb returned to the Whig fold under Charles Grey, serving as Home Secretary from 1830 to 1834.

In 1805 Lamb married Lady Caroline Ponsonby, daughter of the 3rd Earl of Bessborough. This match lasted until their separation in 1825 when the relationship became irreconcilable. They had one son who survived birth but he was severely mentally handicapped and died young. Caroline conducted a notorious relationship with the poet Lord Byron (once slashing her wrists in romantic frustration), while her husband conducted equally scandalous affairs with several married women, including Lady Branden, wife of a clergyman, and Caroline Norton, wife of a lawyer. Both of these affairs required Lamb's defence in divorce suits. All of this came after numerous rumours of Lamb's mother conducting heated affairs with such notables as the Prince of Wales (the future George IV) and Lord Egremont (who some supposed to be Lamb's real father).

Another, quite different, relationship with a woman that Lamb happily cultivated was with the young Queen Victoria, whose political education he oversaw. Lamb (by now Viscount Melbourne) delighted in helping to acquaint the young queen with the protocols and routines that would be required during her reign. This fatherly relationship with her first Prime Minister seemed quite agreeable to Victoria, who found Lamb's personality and approach preferable to some of her later PMs whom she found stuffy, tedious, and distant.

Melbourne's first term as Prime Minister was short, less than a year, taking over after Charles Grey's resignation following the bitter and dramatic passage of the Great Reform Bill of 1832. Like Grey, Melbourne was unable to maintain a balance between those calling for more reform and those wishing to absorb the reforms that had been won. His administration was short-lived, replaced by Sir Robert Peel and the Tories. However, a new party, the Liberal Party, was now emerging out of those like-minded reformers and radicals who sought greater changes in the areas of suffrage, social welfare, and Church reform. Many of these issues involved the more liberal wing of the Tory Party, led by Peel, which was evolving in its own way into the Conservative Party. Indeed, the entire political framework of parliamentary and constitutional monarchy was undergoing enormous change, just as the social and industrial landscape was also being dramatically and rapidly revolutionised.

Melbourne's second administration featured several continued liberal pursuits and accomplishments: the Municipal Reform Act of 1835; granting greater voting privileges in local elections; the suspension of the Jamaican constitution to counter the resistance of local planters to the elimination of slavery; and the ongoing attempt to repeal the Corn Laws. Ironically, the latter goal would be achieved in concert with Whig Party support under the forthcoming Tory government of Peel. More and more, political divisions were being based on the unfolding dynamics of society and the new industrial and economic realities of the nineteenth century.

Melbourne straddled this complicated era, from the age of the Regency of George III's reign to the mid-nineteenth century industrial and social revolutions. No wonder he felt so comfortable spending hours of his premiership each day chatting with and educating the young Queen Victoria rather than debating with Parliament and politicians over the contentious issues of the time. Always a charming and congenial man, Melbourne was best-suited to this role. He became well known throughout the British Empire, and Melbourne, the capital of the state of Victoria in Australia, is named after him.

William Lamb, Lord Melbourne, resigned as PM in 1841, but continued to be a valued and trusted mentor to the Queen. His political career ended in 1842 when he suffered a severe stroke. He died in 1848 and is buried in St Etheldreda's church, next door to Hatfield House, Hertfordshire.

The young Queen Victoria. During her reign (1837–1901), she was served by ten different PMs.

SIR ROBERT PEEL

Born: 5 February 1788
Died: 2 July 1850
Party: Tory
Served: 10 December 1834 – 8 April 1835
30 August 1841 – 29 June 1846
(6 years, 255 days)

"Of all the vulgar acts of Government, that of solving every difficulty by thrusting the hand into the public purse is the most contemptible"

Sir Robert Peel was twice Prime Minister, serving first under King William IV and then under Queen Victoria. Peel was born in 1788, the son of Sir Robert Peel and Ellen Yates. Educated at Oxford, Peel entered Parliament in 1809 and served as Under-Secretary of State for War and Colonies in the government of Spencer Perceval. When Robert Jenkinson (Lord Liverpool) became PM he chose Peel, only twenty-four years old, as Secretary for Ireland. Peel's influence would go on to have a profound effect that resonates to this day. If nothing else, whenever one refers to a policeman as a 'Bobby' it is a tribute to Peel's formation of the Metropolitan Police.

Appointed Home Secretary in 1822, Peel pursued the reform and streamlining of the criminal law codes. Later, in concert with the Duke of Wellington, Peel tackled urban crime by establishing the Metropolitan Police to attempt a method of organised law enforcement over the rapidly and ever-growing capital city. These 'Peelers' or 'Bobbies' soon set the example for police forces all over the world.

Peel's reputation as an opponent of Catholic emancipation had been well known since he had exercised Cabinet responsibility for Ireland (where he was known as 'Orange Peel'). The bitter split in the Tory Party over this question had divided several Tory Cabinets into Protestant and pro-Catholic wings. However, in 1829, under the direction and support of Wellington as PM and with Peel as Leader of the House of Commons, Catholic emancipation was eventually enshrined in law. This seeming betrayal by two former staunch opponents of emancipation led to deep bitterness and resentment within the Protestant wing of the party, costing Peel his parliamentary seat in the next election. But it certainly demonstrated willingness on the part of Peel and

Wellington to compromise on an issue of intense emotional division for the good of the nation.

During Peel's first term as Prime Minister (1834–35) he issued the Tamworth Manifesto, which outlined the objectives of his party – more and more viewed as the 'Conservative' Party. In fact, Peel is the last PM to be classified as 'Tory,' though the Conservative Party has retained 'Tory' as its nickname. Peel later became Prime Minister a second time (1841–46) with a much stronger majority and pursued policies that many considered to be liberal. His dedication to the repeal of the Corn Laws (tariffs on grain) deeply upset many within his own party and passage of the necessary legislation only came about through strong liberal support from the opposition Whigs. Peel's progressive approach to reform did not sit well with the large conservative element within his own party, and, immediately following the repeal of the Corn Laws, Peel's administration was brought down by a combined Whig and conservative Tory vote. Peel's career in government came to an end as he never held office again.

He had in 1820 married Julia Floyd, daughter of General Sir John Floyd, and was devoted to his family. He was a trustee of the British Museum and collected fine art that he later donated to the nation. A great believer in science and industry, Peel fully supported the new system of railways that was revolutionizing the country.

In the summer of 1850, Peel was thrown from his horse while riding in Hyde Park and died four days later on 2 July 1850. He is buried in St Peter's church, Drayton Bassett, Staffordshire, near the grounds of what was once his family estate.

There has always been a debate as to what degree Peel inspired the modern Conservative Party. He definitely influenced the evolution of the Tories into the Conservatives, and his liberal-leaning policies helped send party members in two directions. Many 'Peelites', such as William Gladstone, merged with the remnants of the Whigs and Radicals to form the Liberal Party, while those Tories who felt betrayed by Peel, such as Benjamin Disraeli, went on to form the Conservative Party. Britain had arrived at a watershed in its political history, with Sir Robert Peel playing no small part.

A statue of Peel in the town of his birth, Bury.

JOHN RUSSELL

EARL RUSSELL

Born:	18 August 1792
Died:	28 May 1878
Party:	Whig / Liberal
Served:	30 June 1846 – 21 February 1852
	29 October 1865 – 26 June 1866
	(6 years, 11 days)

*"I have made mistakes,
but in all I did, my object was
the public good"*

JOHN RUSSELL was twice Prime Minister under Queen Victoria. He was the third son of John Russell, 6th Duke of Bedford, and Georgiana Byng. Russell was educated at Edinburgh University and entered Parliament in 1813, inheriting his family's Whig politics, but not much of their considerable fortune. His lifetime commitment was to parliamentary reform. Prime Minister Charles Grey chose Russell to help draft and introduce the Great Reform Bill of 1832. Russell worked tirelessly during the difficult and eventually successful passage of the landmark legislation. He had ability, energy, and determination in furthering the aspirations and philosophical doctrines that were to define the emerging Liberal Party then evolving from the liberal wings of the older Whig and Tory parties.

Russell became Home Secretary and later Colonial Secretary under Whig Prime Minister William Lamb (Viscount Melbourne). When Sir Robert Peel and the Tories regained power in 1841, Russell supported Peel's successful efforts to finally repeal the Corn Laws. Ironically, Peel's success spelled the end of his own administration and opened the door for the Whigs to regain power under Russell's leadership. As Prime Minister, Russell now relied on the support of opposition leader Peel, reversing the former situation. The two parties continued splintering into factions that would eventually coalesce into the respective Liberal and Conservative parties.

Russell's first administration produced liberal reform laws concerning limitations on the working day (1847) and the Public Health Act to provide for better sewers and drains (1848). It also witnessed the rise in popularity and reputation of Russell's chief rival, Foreign Secretary Henry Temple (Viscount Palmerston). In December 1851 Russell dismissed Palmerston for taking it upon himself to recognise France's controversial new regime led by Napoleon III. But Palmerston was not going to go away, and as Russell's political stature diminished, Palmerston's only increased. Just three months later, in February 1852, Russell and the Whigs were defeated in Parliament – with no little help from Palmerston – and Russell resigned. Palmerston, at the head of the new Liberal Party, would go on to serve twice as Prime Minister, while Russell would only regain the position when Palmerston died in office in 1865.

The rivalry between Palmerston and Russell continued within the confines of the new Liberal Party, carrying on until Palmerston's death. Queen Victoria, no fan of either, called them 'those two dreadful old men'. Russell's brief second term as Prime Minister, now under the banner of the Liberal Party, again sought greater political and social reforms, but his administration lacked traction and he resigned in June 1866, just eight months after resuming the top job. He would not hold office again.

Russell had married in 1835 Adelaide Lister, widow of Lord Ribblesdale. The couple had two daughters before Adelaide died in 1838. He then married Frances Eliot, daughter of the 2nd Earl of Minto, and produced four more children. His grandson, Bertrand Russell, became a well-known philosopher in the twentieth century.

Though instrumental in the passing of the Great Reform Bill of 1832, John Russell's two terms as Prime Minister were not particularly successful. Queen Victoria called him 'peevish Johnny' as he was well known for his grumbling, pettiness, and lack of tact, but his determination and vision on liberal issues and reforms were significant, setting the stage for the great Liberal Party reforms under William Gladstone in the second half of the nineteenth century.

Russell was created 1st Earl Russell in 1861. He died in 1878 and is buried in the Duke of Bedford's family mausoleum at St Michael's church, Chenies, Buckinghamshire. The church is open to the public, but the interior of the magnificent mausoleum, though visible through windows, is restricted to family members.

Chartist rally on Kennington Common, 10 April 1848. This put Russell as Prime Minister in a difficult position, since he had always championed freedom of speech and wider suffrage. Fearful of a riot, Russell allowed the meeting to go ahead on the understanding that the Chartists would not march on Parliament with their petition. Thousands of soldiers and special constables were also on duty that day to ensure order.

EDWARD SMITH-STANLEY

EARL OF DERBY

Born: 29 March 1799
Died: 23 October 1869
Party: Conservative
Served: 23 February 1852 – 17 December 1852
20 February 1858 – 11 June 1859
28 June 1866 – 25 February 1868
(3 years, 280 days)

Considered the father of the modern Conservative Party, his leadership of the party lasted for twenty-two years

EDWARD SMITH-STANLEY, 14th Earl of Derby, was Prime Minister three times during the reign of Queen Victoria. His administrations were the first to represent the Conservative Party, a group that had descended from the old Tory Party, but which had a new agenda of political, social, and foreign policy doctrine.

Stanley was born in 1799, heir to one of Britain's richest and most famous titles. The eldest son of Edward Smith-Stanley, 13th Earl of Derby, and Charlotte Margaret Hornby, Stanley was educated at Eton and Oxford and entered Parliament in 1822. As a strong supporter of the landed gentry, Stanley followed a political path that attempted to protect what he felt was the backbone of Britain, the English landowning class. In so doing, Stanley frequently shifted political parties in order to protect and promulgate his political position. In the end, though without explicit intention, he wound up forging a new political entity, the Conservative Party, which has endured to this day.

Stanley began his career as a Whig, throwing in his lot with the traditional establishment grandees. But in 1827 he accepted the position of Under-Secretary of State for War and the Colonies under Tory PM George Canning. He returned to the Whigs when the Tory Duke of Wellington became Prime Minister, and he served in Charles Grey's Whig administration. Stanley received much of the credit for the abolition of slavery while serving as Chief Secretary of Ireland (1830–33) and later as Secretary of State for War and the Colonies (1833–34). Incompatible with Whig Prime Minister John Russell, Stanley resigned, only to reappear in Sir Robert Peel's Tory administration, again holding the ministerial brief for War and the Colonies (1841–44). When Peel successfully repealed the Corn Laws (tariffs on imported grain and dear to the hearts of the great land owners), Stanley felt betrayed and resigned. With no party to associate with, Stanley led a large portion of similar-minded Tories and Whigs to unite as the Conservative Party. Those Whig and Tory reformers of a more progressive persuasion united to form the Liberal Party. Though never planned, nor as neat and tidy as it now might seem in retrospect, the result was the emergence of two political parties of divergent leadership and philosophies.

Derby inherited the title Earl of Derby upon the death of his father in 1851, though he had already accepted a title and moved to the House of Lords in 1844. His leadership role in the Commons eventually went, with his support, to the rising star of the Conservative Party, Benjamin Disraeli, who would go on to further define the Conservative Party in the years to come.

Stanley's three terms as Prime Minister were all brief and without majorities in the Commons. The first, in 1852, lasted but eleven months, coming on the heels of the collapse of the Russell administration. There was little support for Derby's government or his renewed efforts to secure more grain tariffs, so he duly resigned. In February 1858, Derby formed another government, but again the administration lacked broad support and he resigned in June 1859. However, the Derby administration had begun to show a more moderate side to its policies, not least in its willingness to increase the voting franchise, a break from Derby's previously more restrictive view as to who should be allowed the vote. In 1866, though in ill health, the opportunity to once more form a government presented itself to Derby and the Conservatives. Derby and Disraeli, to the chagrin of the Liberals, put forth the Second Reform Bill, further expanding the franchise. When the Liberals salted it with amendments to further increase its reforms, the Conservatives refused to blink. They accepted it, ran with it, and ensured its passage into law in 1867. Plagued by severe and chronic gout, Derby resigned in 1868, turning over party leadership to Disraeli, who had been highly instrumental in the successful passage of the Bill.

Though conservative in his politics and social outlook, Derby was also a true defender of, and provider for, the weak and needy. He contributed significant funds to out-of-work cotton textile workers who had lost their jobs due to the American Civil War. He donated large amounts to the welfare of employees on his land to prevent any of them from having to go to a poorhouse. He employed his personal physician to tend to the sick on his estates and contributed generous amounts to the poor in his London church parish. He certainly played a major part in enlarging the voting franchise during his third stint as PM.

Stanley was a famously powerful speaker, earning praise from no less than the great American orator Daniel Webster. Stanley married Emma Bootle-Wilbraham in 1825 and had two sons and one daughter. Beyond his political career, Stanley was for many years the Chancellor of Oxford University and a noted classical scholar in his own right. He was also Steward of the Jockey Club, horse-racing being his lifelong passion. Despite spending a small fortune on his stable, his horses never won his namesake race, the Derby. He was quite ill during his third premiership, resigning in 1868 and giving way to Disraeli. He died in 1869 and is buried in the crypt of St Mary's church, Knowsley, Lancashire. Disraeli summed up Derby's career when he said, 'Derby abolished slavery, educated Ireland, and reformed Parliament.'

GEORGE HAMILTON-GORDON

EARL OF ABERDEEN

Born: 28 January 1784
Died: 14 December 1860
Party: Tory / Peelite
Served: 19 December 1852 – 30 January 1855
(2 years, 42 days)

"I do not know how I shall bear being out of office … After being occupied with great affairs, it is not easy to subside to the level of common occupations"

GEORGE HAMILTON-GORDON was Prime Minister under Queen Victoria in the mid-nineteenth century. Gordon's background and forte was foreign policy, serving as he did in numerous foreign and diplomatic capacities within several administrations. His foreign policy goal was to maintain the peace of Europe following the Napoleonic Wars. Ironically, on becoming Prime Minister, Gordon oversaw Great Britain's involvement in the Crimean War, as France and Britain defended the declining Ottoman Empire in its war with Russia. The controversy over Britain's military conduct, and the domestic outrage at her lack of preparation concerning the war, led to the collapse of Gordon's government and ended his heretofore successful public career, leaving him deeply depressed and in ill health.

Gordon was born in 1784, the son of George Gordon and Charlotte Baird. Following the deaths of his father (1791) and mother (1795), he was adopted by William Pitt the Younger and Scottish politician Henry Dundas (Viscount Melville). He was educated at Harrow and Cambridge, and inherited the title of Earl of Aberdeen upon the death of his grandfather in 1801, assuming a seat in the House of Lords.

Aberdeen had four children from his first marriage to Catherine Hamilton in 1805; sadly, his wife died in 1812. Sorrow plagued him, as their son died in infancy and all three of his daughters died before they were twenty. In 1815 he married Harriet Douglas, the widow of his first wife's brother, Viscount James Hamilton. They had four sons and one daughter.

Aberdeen served as Foreign Secretary in the Tory governments of both the Duke of Wellington and Sir Robert Peel. He was Ambassador to Austria under Lord Liverpool and later negotiated several treaties with the United States, including the establishment of permanent borders with areas of what today is Canada. He also negotiated the Oregon Treaty of 1846 between Britain and the US.

Aberdeen was called upon to form a coalition government in late 1852. He attempted to unite his fellow Peelite Tories with the reforming Whigs under John Russell and Viscount Palmerston. However, by 1854 Britain was embroiled in the Crimean War against Russia. This war featured modern advances such as steamships, the telegraph, and increasingly more powerful and accurate muskets and artillery. The new and revolutionary 'on the scene' presence and rapid reporting of war conditions by correspondents, such as the *Times* reporter W. H. Russell, gave the war a distinctly modern flavour and opened the door for criticism of the government's handling of the war. Disasters such as the reckless and doomed 'Charge of the Light Brigade', along with the humanitarian work done by Florence Nightingale to ease the pain of wounded soldiers who were suffering under horribly inadequate medical care, all gave rise to bitter public outcry. Aberdeen, as head of the government, bore the brunt of these attacks and he resigned in 1855. His health continued to deteriorate and he did not hold office again.

Made a Knight of the Thistle in 1805 and Knight of the Garter in 1845, George Hamilton-Gordon died in 1860, never recovering either his confidence or his health. Buried at the Church of St John the Evangelist in Stanmore, Middlesex, this British Prime Minister has a lovely effigy in the new church, but his family vault is in the backyard crypt beneath the ruins of the old church.

An 1855 print from the Crimean War, depicting war-weary soldiers in search of warmth and shelter. The outcry over terrible conditions contributed to the Earl of Aberdeen's resignation.

HENRY TEMPLE

VISCOUNT PALMERSTON

Born: 20 October 1784
Died: 18 October 1865
Party: Liberal
Served: 6 February 1855 – 19 February 1858
            12 June 1859 – 18 October 1865
            (9 years, 141 days)

"Nations have no permanent friends or allies: they only have permanent interests"

HENRY JOHN TEMPLE was twice Prime Minister of Great Britain under Queen Victoria. He died in office at the age of eighty-one, less than six months after a successful re-election campaign. He served in various high capacities of government for nearly six decades. His political arrangement with John Russell, William Gladstone (both Victorian Prime Ministers), and the more liberal elements of the former Whig and Tory parties, is generally considered to have formed the Liberal Party.

Temple was born in 1784 at the estate of Broadlands – the future home and estate of Lord Louis Mountbatten. He was the son of Henry and Mary Temple, inheriting the title of 3rd Viscount Palmerston upon the death of his father in 1802. He was educated at Harrow and Cambridge, and entered Parliament in 1807. Palmerston began a nineteen-year stint as Secretary at War, serving in various governments before entering the Cabinet in 1827. He served as Foreign Secretary on four different occasions, again in numerous administrations. His competence in office was recognised by many, though his party affiliation frequently wandered back and forth between the Tories and Whigs. He demonstrated a fiercely independent personality, quarrelling frequently with foes and allies alike. As Prime Ministers, Palmerston and the equally irascible John ('peevish Johnny') Russell were referred to by Queen Victoria as 'those two dreadful old men'.

His behaviour, philosophy, accomplishments, and varied sense of political identity make him a difficult man to label as he bounded all over the political and social map. He may have lived in Victorian times, but a stereotypical Victorian he was not. He was rude and abrasive to many, acquiring the nickname 'Lord Pumicestone', but he also took a decidedly light-hearted attitude toward governing that appeared jaunty and, according to Disraeli, at times 'rollicking'. He had large appetites for food, ladies, and horses. He was accused by an irate Queen Victoria of attempting to seduce one of her ladies-in-waiting at Windsor Castle, and he was involved in a divorce case at age seventy-nine. He did not marry until he was fifty-five, waiting until his long-time mistress Emily Lamb (Lady Cowper) – sister of PM William Lamb (Viscount Melbourne) – had been widowed by the death of her husband. They had no children, although one of Emily's daughters was always rumoured to be Palmerston's. Perhaps not surprisingly, Palmerston saw the Bill of Matrimonial Causes passed in 1857 which allowed courts to grant a divorce, changing what had long been a church jurisdiction.

Palmerston had become Prime Minister in 1855 during the Crimean War, and at the age of seventy he remains the oldest person to take up the premiership for the first time. The widely publicised harsh conditions experienced by the British Army, along with military setbacks, had brought down the government of George Hamilton-Gordon (Earl of Aberdeen). In early 1856 Palmerston negotiated an armistice and brought the war to a close.

A confirmed abolitionist, it would have seemed inconsistent to support the pro-slavery Southern Confederacy during the American Civil War, but Palmerston was never friendly to the ideals and goals of the United States and was normally hostile to the US. However, though sympathetic to the cotton-producing social class of the Southern states, he never deviated from his strict anti-slavery position and maintained neutrality throughout the war.

With the exception of a few months' government by Lord Derby's Conservative Party, Palmerston remained in office as Prime Minister for close to ten years. During this time Britain experienced prosperity and technological advancements. Global economic and colonial expansion increased, and Britain's position as a world leader was reinforced. Palmerston was able to mesh the liberal fragments of the exhausted Tory Party with similarly minded remnants of the Whigs to form the Liberal Party that would pursue and enact the reform of British politics for the next sixty years.

Henry Temple, Lord Palmerston, died in 1865 and was the last Prime Minister to die in office. He had requested burial at Romsey Abbey but instead was given a state funeral and buried with high honours at Westminster Abbey.

BENJAMIN DISRAELI

Born: 21 December 1804
Died: 19 April 1881
Party: Conservative
Served: 27 February 1868 – 1 December 1868
20 February 1874 – 21 April 1880
(6 years, 339 days)

*"My idea of an agreeable person is
a person who agrees with me"*

BENJAMIN DISRAELI served two terms as Prime Minister. Famous for overcoming the prejudices of the time about his Jewish ancestry, Disraeli was a political curiosity: a failed author, born without family pedigree, and lacking any prior social or political base. Despite these obstacles, Disraeli was able to climb what he described as the 'greasy pole' of politics to the top. He exuded a very great deal of persistence, vanity and ambition, reflected in a personality that charmed some and disgusted others. A romantic believer in the glory of the British Empire, he oversaw the creation of Queen Victoria as Empress of India and obtained for Britain a large interest in Egypt's Suez Canal. Disraeli not only dominated the political stage, but the social one as well, relishing the role of Victorian dandy with his penchant for flamboyant dress and manners. As Prime Minister, he endlessly flattered the Queen and became her enthusiastic champion. In Parliament, he demonstrated a talent for brilliant debate, but he also found time to write several novels while maintaining a well-earned reputation as a bon vivant throughout the parlours of Victorian society. 'When I want to read a novel, I write one,' he was famously quoted as saying. Self-confidence he did not lack.

Disraeli was born in London, the eldest son of Issac and Maria (*née* Basevi) D'Israeli. Though of Jewish background, Benjamin's father had his son baptised as a Christian in the Church of England. Educated at home and local schools, Disraeli became the first complete 'outsider' to rise to the top of British politics, lacking as he did title, inherited land, or an education at a famous university. His early interests were world travel and writing, concentrating first on articles for newspapers before becoming a novelist. He continued writing novels well into his seventies. In his youth he enjoyed assuming the role of a rake and a radical both in dress and manner, collecting a well-deserved reputation as a London society dandy.

Disraeli turned to politics and entered Parliament in 1837, though it took five attempts before he was elected. He excelled as a speaker and his speeches in opposition to Sir Robert Peel's desire to repeal the Corn Laws split the Tory Party and brought Disraeli recognition. It also began the formation of the Conservative Party under Edward Smith-Stanley (Earl of Derby). Since Derby served in the House of Lords, Disraeli assumed the leadership of the Conservatives in the Commons. Eventually, Derby was to become Prime Minister three times, with Disraeli serving as his Chancellor of the Exchequer on each occasion.

After several well-publicised affairs, Disraeli settled down and married the wealthy widow Mary Anne Wyndham Lewis, twelve years his senior. It was a happy marriage and Disraeli was devastated by her death in 1872. They had no children. He purchased an estate, Hughenden Manor, and became a country gentleman.

Lord Derby's third administration saw the passage of the Second Reform Bill (1867), which Disraeli steered through Parliament, resulting in the near doubling of the eligible electorate. It was more liberal than William Gladstone's Liberal Party reform bill, which failed to pass, refuting the notion that the Conservatives were opposed to political reform. This further increased the rising animosity between Gladstone and Disraeli. The two bitterly opposed political warriors were to square off again and again in their parliamentary debates.

Disraeli became Prime Minister in 1868 when illness forced Derby to retire. It was a short administration since Gladstone and the Liberals won the general election later that same year. But the Disraeli-led Conservatives returned to office in 1874 and Disraeli became Prime Minister again – this time for six years. His second term featured social and industrial reforms ranging from education and public health to allowing peaceful picketing by trade unions. Disraeli sought to identify the Conservative Party with a sense of civic consciousness.

At this time he also enhanced the globe-straddling British Empire. The purchase of the Suez Canal and the creation of Queen Victoria as Empress of India, framed against the backdrop of the *Pax Britannica*, underscored Britain's position as one of the world's economic and military powerhouses.

Disraeli was made the 1st Earl of Beaconsfield in 1876. He remained Prime Minister until 1880, when Gladstone and the Liberal Party returned to power. He died in 1881 and is buried beside his wife at St Michael's church on the grounds of his Hughenden estate. Queen Victoria showed her deep respect for Disraeli by later visiting Hughenden and laying flowers on his grave.

WILLIAM GLADSTONE

Born:	29 December 1809
Died:	19 May 1898
Party:	Liberal
Served:	3 December 1868 – 17 Feb. 1874
	23 April 1880 – 9 June 1885
	1 February 1886 – 20 July 1886
	15 August 1892 – 2 March 1894
	(12 years, 126 days)

"Justice delayed is justice denied"

WILLIAM EWART GLADSTONE served as Prime Minister under Queen Victoria on four separate occasions. He was a major player in British and world politics for over fifty years, dominating the domestic political stage for the greater part of the later nineteenth century through the sheer momentum of his personal and philosophical convictions. His forceful personality, relentless energy, and strident belief in the righteous necessity to improve society lent an almost religious zeal to the reforms he pursued to restructure British society.

Gladstone was born in Liverpool in 1809. His father was Sir John Gladstone, a man of ardent religious beliefs who encouraged William to seriously consider the priesthood as a vocation. But, having been schooled at Eton and Christ Church, Oxford, he entered politics in 1832 as a Tory Member of Parliament, and was chosen by Prime Minister Sir Robert Peel for positions at the Board of Trade, eventually becoming its President. In these posts he not only excelled, but also developed a strong regard for the benefits of free trade.

Peel died following a horse-riding accident in 1850, leaving Gladstone and other so-called 'Peelites' with a decision to make about their political future. Gladstone spent the 1850s wavering between leading his fellow Peelites into the emerging Liberal Party or the evolving Conservative Party, the nascent political entities that were replacing the former Whig and Tory factions. He rejected the Conservatives due to their protectionist trade policies, as well as his personal dislike of Conservative leader Benjamin Disraeli. Overcoming many doubts about Lord Palmerston and his Liberal government, Gladstone found refuge in their policy of reduced taxes and chose the Liberal Party as the vehicle for his future political journey.

During the 1860s, Gladstone became leader of the Liberal Party in Parliament and campaigned and established himself as the reforming champion of the common people. He remained in the Liberal government after Palmerston's death in 1865, and with the defeat of the Conservatives in 1868 Gladstone commenced the first of his four terms as Prime Minister. His premiership featured numerous social and political reforms: an Education Act that made elementary education available to children aged five to thirteen; an anti-flogging act for the armed forces; the Ballot Act of 1872 for the allowance of secret ballots in local and general elections; and an Irish Land Act (the Irish question always being close to Gladstone's heart) that provided greater security from eviction and rent increase.

The Liberal Party's reform agenda ran out of steam in 1874, and Gladstone's arch rival, Disraeli, came to power for the next six years. When Gladstone returned as Prime Minister in 1880, he was plagued by foreign policy setbacks in South Africa, Egypt and Sudan. The later conflict resulted in the humiliating and tragic defeat and death of General Charles Gordon at the Battle of Khartoum in 1885. In this matter, Gladstone was held personally responsible for failing to promptly reinforce Gordon's doomed outpost in time to save his life, earning Gladstone the title 'Murderer of Gordon'.

Gladstone never enjoyed the sort of warm relationship with Queen Victoria that his great Tory rival cultivated. Disraeli, whether in or out of office, championed the Queen and the glory of the British Empire, thereby securing Victoria's favour and respect. Gladstone ridiculed Disraeli's elevating the Queen to Empress of India, and claimed Disraeli was a pretender, finding both his domestic and foreign policies to be out of date and foolish. Victoria never appreciated Gladstone on a personal level, did not relish his urging her to make more public appearances, and deeply resented his implying her illnesses were more imagined than real. His lack of success in foreign policy, in particular the embarrassment over Gordon's death, only further undermined his position with the Queen.

In his personal life, Gladstone had eight children by his wife Catherine Glynne. His happy and successful marriage, which also brought him Hawarden Castle in Wales, contrasts with his unusual habit of walking the streets of London in search of prostitutes in need of reclamation. This preoccupation with converting ladies of the night into righteous and law-abiding citizens seemed bizarre to even his closest friends, but Gladstone persisted in this peculiar behaviour until 1886 when he was seventy-five.

Gladstone's fourth term as Prime Minister came in 1892–94 and saw passage of the bill for Irish Home Rule. This had been his foremost objective during his short-lived third term (1886) and remained a dominating issue for the rest of his career. Unfortunately for Gladstone, the issue had split the Liberal Party in 1886, and even when passed in 1893, the bill was defeated in the House of Lords. After admitting defeat on this and other pet issues, an exhausted Gladstone resigned at age eighty-three.

Though no longer in political favour, Gladstone was recognised for his great contributions to liberal reform and his impressive personal rectitude. He died of cancer in 1898 at the age of eighty-nine. He was buried with full honours in Westminster Abbey, having outlived his rival Benjamin Disraeli by seventeen years. Two future kings served as pallbearers: Edward, Prince of Wales, and George, Duke of York.

ROBERT GASCOYNE-CECIL

MARQUESS OF SALISBURY

Born:	3 February 1830
Died:	22 August 1903
Party:	Conservative
Served:	23 June 1885 – 28 January 1886
	25 July 1886 – 11 August 1892
	25 June 1895 – 11 July 1902
	(13 years, 252 days)

"If I were asked to define Conservative policy, I should say that it was the upholding of confidence"

ROBERT GASCOYNE-CECIL was descended from both William and Robert Cecil, the famous and respected chief ministers to sixteenth- and seventeenth-century monarchs Elizabeth I and James I. Following in their successful footsteps, Cecil became Prime Minister on three occasions under Queen Victoria. He enjoyed the challenge of politics, but was essentially a scholarly and shy man, preferring to remain if possible at Hatfield House, his family's stately ancestral Hertfordshire manor. Cecil was the last Prime Minister to govern from the House of Lords, having inherited his distinguished title upon the death of his father, the 2nd Marquess of Salisbury, in 1868.

The son of James Gascoyne-Cecil and Frances (*née* Gascoyne), Robert was educated at Eton and Oxford, though at Eton he was withdrawn from school due to incessant bullying. He had a passion for scholarly and practical interests that included botany, physics, theology, and photography. Indeed, under Cecil's forward-minded encouragement, Hatfield House became one of the first great manor houses to be electrically illuminated. Earlier, in 1857, Cecil had married Georgina Alderton (going on to produce a family of five sons and three daughters). This match was quite against his father's wishes, and the resultant financial abandonment required Cecil to earn a meagre income through journalism. Cecil was very religious and deeply conservative in his world outlook: socially, politically, and philosophically. This was to dictate much of his politics and policies as Prime Minister. He entered Parliament in 1853 and began to assume financial independence in 1865 when he became heir to the Salisbury title after the death of his elder brother.

Cecil opposed most reform and resigned from the Cabinet when the Second Reform Bill was passed under a Conservative government led by Lord Derby. He was wary of increased democracy, strongly favoured the Church of England, and opposed Jews gaining membership to the House of Commons. He was in favour of religious tests for entry into Cambridge and Oxford, and he disliked Prime Minister Benjamin Disraeli, even though he was a fellow Tory. Yet in addition to his staunch conservatism he was a practical politician who was able to harness wide support by capitalizing upon Disraeli's success at producing and promoting a greater British Empire and by accepting and adapting to reforms in order to benefit the Conservative Party. His political instincts made him adept at recognizing and exploiting serious splits in the Liberal Party, which produced election victories for the Conservatives.

Salisbury, as he became known from 1868, enjoyed the conduct of foreign policy and while serving as Prime Minister he also held the office of Foreign Secretary for twelve of his nearly fourteen years in the top job. His policies promoted peace and economic restraint, factors that he felt went hand in hand. His administrations produced social improvements in working-class housing and free elementary education (1891). He believed in patience as the most effective method to either amplify positive results or to retard negative effects. While unsupportive of the growing power of an increased electorate, he accepted its inevitability. He feared and respected the growing strength of Germany while attempting to blunt its ramifications.

During his third term his health declined and his interest grew more detached. Britain's ill-advised South African policy resulted in the bitter Boer War and soured his final years in office. Upon a general election victory in 1900, coupled with an acceptable conclusion to the Boer War, Salisbury was able to turn the premiership over to his nephew, Arthur Balfour, in 1902.

Retiring from the political stage, he died in 1903 and is buried in the Cecil family plot at his Hatfield House estate, which rests beside St Etheldreda's church in Hertfordshire.

ARCHIBALD PRIMROSE

EARL OF ROSEBERY

Born: 7 May 1847
Died: 21 May 1929
Party: Liberal
Served: 5 March 1894 – 22 June 1895
           (1 year, 109 days)

*"The British Empire is a
Commonwealth of Nations"*

ARCHIBALD PRIMROSE served a brief sixteen months as Prime Minister, succeeding William Gladstone, who resigned in 1894. Primrose had served under Gladstone in several capacities, including Foreign Secretary, and was an immediate contender to succeed him. His only competition came from the difficult and troublesome Sir William Harcourt, who, though certainly qualified, was not favoured by either his fellow Liberals or Queen Victoria. This allowed Primrose to assume the premiership.

The eldest son of Archibald (Lord Dalmeny) and Catherine (*née* Stanhope) Primrose, young Archibald attended Eton and Christ Church, Oxford, where he was expelled for racing his horses – one of his lifelong passions. In fact, early on he proclaimed three great wishes in life: to win the Derby, marry a rich wife, and become Prime Minister. He would fully accomplish all of his goals. Born to Scottish wealth, Primrose inherited numerous estates; his father, Lord Dalmeny, had died young in 1850, and Primrose became Earl of Rosebery upon the death of his grandfather in 1868.

In 1878, Rosebery married Hannah de Rothschild, heiress to a large part of the Rothschild fortune. They had four children – two sons and two daughters. At the same time, Primrose was vigorously supporting William Gladstone and the Liberal Party, while building his own reputation. His horses won the Derby three times and he enjoyed a steady climb up the Liberal Party ladder while serving in the Gladstone government. Unfortunately, Hannah died in 1890, leaving Rosebery grief-stricken. His enduring disputes with Harcourt, both before and during his tenure as Prime Minister, were a constant hindrance, personally and politically. His term in office was plagued by party infighting, lack of any kind of agreement in his Cabinet, and an overall inability to co-ordinate policy on either domestic or foreign affairs. The Liberals were soundly defeated by the Conservatives in the 1895 general election, and no one was happier than Rosebery to give up the reins of office.

As a Liberal Prime Minister and as leader in opposition, Rosebery was equally unsuccessful. On issues ranging from Irish Home Rule (he postponed it), to support for Britain's colonial empire in Africa (he broke with Gladstone), and the controversial matter of his erecting a statue of Oliver Cromwell outside Parliament, he proved awkward and inept.

Rosebery gradually distanced himself from government, concentrating on his horses and the writing of several biographies of eminent men such as Cromwell and both William Pitts. He died in 1929 and was buried in the family vault at Dalmeny church in Scotland.

Archibald Primrose, Lord Rosebery, was bright, intelligent, and socially charming, but the halls of power were difficult for him to successfully navigate and he seemed to sense it with a later comment: 'There are two supreme pleasures in life ... The ideal is when a man receives the seals of office ... The real pleasure comes when he hands them back.'

Rosebery as a younger man in a *Vanity Fair* caricature of 1876. Reflecting his equine obsession, the caption was simply 'Horses'.

ARTHUR BALFOUR

Born: 25 July 1848
Died: 19 March 1930
Party: Conservative
Served: 11 July 1902 – 5 December 1905
         (3 years, 145 days)

*"Nothing matters very much, and
very few things matter at all"*

ARTHUR JAMES BALFOUR figured prominently in a wide array of significant events that dramatically bridge his own period to the present. His degree of personal influence in these decisions has been open to debate, but the global impact of the events is without question. With a political career spanning over fifty years, which included more than three as Prime Minister, Balfour held ministerial positions that involved him in not only the alliance with France that evolved into the Triple Entente and entry into the First World War, but also the controversial 'Balfour Declaration' of 1917, which supported the establishment of a homeland for Jewish emigrants and settlers in what is now the modern state of Israel. He also coined the oft-repeated, cynically clever phrase, 'Nothing matters very much, and few things matter at all.'

Born to wealth and position in Whittingehame, East Lothian, Balfour was the eldest son of James Maitland Balfour and Lady Blanche Cecil, daughter of the 2nd Marquess of Salisbury. This family connection would make Balfour a nephew of future three-time Prime Minister Robert Gascoyne-Cecil (3rd Marquess of Salisbury) and provide a strong boost to his own political career. Educated at Eton and Trinity College, Cambridge, Balfour studied philosophy, writing two books on the subject. A sports enthusiast, he captained the Royal and Ancient Golf Club of St Andrews and played vigorous tennis into his late years. Reflecting his ease of presence within the emerging twentieth century, Balfour became the first Prime Minister to drive a car to No. 10 Downing Street. A lifelong bachelor, he had been engaged to May Lyttleton who died of typhoid fever in 1875, and though continuing to enjoy the company of women, he never seemed to overcome the grief of her early death.

Balfour first entered Parliament in 1874, his position within the Conservative Party enhanced by the support of his uncle, Lord Salisbury. He became Secretary for Ireland in 1887, earning the nickname 'Bloody Balfour' for his firm and often ruthless execution of British policy. Ironically, Balfour later spearheaded several Irish reform acts, including the Irish Local Government Act of 1898, providing some relief to the chronically troubling issues of Irish policy. By 1891 he had already advanced to First Lord of the Treasury, becoming the last holder of that office not in combination with the premiership. Assuming the rank of Leader of the House of Commons, Balfour earned a reputation as a brilliant and effective speaker, thus setting the stage for him to succeed Lord Salisbury as Prime Minister. The ailing and weary Salisbury retired in 1902, prompting Balfour's elevation to PM.

The Conservative Party was bitterly divided by squabbles over free trade and the waging of the Boer War in South Africa. Balfour attempted to defer debate on the trade issue and avoid further division. But the trade issue led to numerous resignations within his Cabinet and the ongoing debate eroded the strength of his administration. The Boer War was resolved in 1902 on terms that proved satisfactory enough for Salisbury to retire, though the South African conflict had revealed grave military inefficiencies and Balfour used this as a springboard for long-neglected reform and rearmament.

In foreign affairs, Balfour desired to provide Britain with a strategic ally on the continent of Europe, and this pursuit would have enormous consequences for the future. The threat posed by the growing military and economic strength of Germany would lead to his endorsement of a treaty with France, the 'Entente Cordiale' of 1904, which later included Tsarist Russia in a three-nation alliance (the so-called Triple Entente) that would drag Britain into the nightmare of the First World War.

The general election of 1906 brought a defeat of large and embarrassing proportions as Balfour and the Conservatives were swept out of office. Balfour remained leader of the Conservatives until resigning in 1911. He returned to high office during the First World War as First Lord of the Admiralty, replacing Winston Churchill following the Gallipoli disaster. After supporting David Lloyd George's bid to remove Herbert Asquith from the premiership, Balfour was named Foreign Secretary. It was in this position in 1917 that he issued the far-reaching Balfour Declaration, calling for a Jewish homeland in Palestine.

Balfour served in the House of Commons until 1922, and was made 1st Earl Balfour the same year. He played a role at several international conferences under Prime Minister Stanley Baldwin during the 1920s. He died in 1930 and is buried in the family plot of the Balfour estate of Whittingehame, near Haddington, Scotland.

SIR HENRY CAMPBELL-BANNERMAN

Born:	7 September 1836
Died:	22 April 1908
Party:	Liberal
Served:	5 December 1905 – 7 April 1908
	(2 years 122 days)

> *"Personally I am an immense believer in bed, in constantly keeping horizontal: the heart and everything else goes slower, and the whole system is refreshed"*

SIR HENRY CAMPBELL-BANNERMAN served as Prime Minister under King Edward VII. Born Henry Campbell in 1836, he took the name of Bannerman upon inheritance of his uncle's estate in 1868. He was actually the first Prime Minister to be officially called 'Prime Minister' and the first to emerge from the world of business. He died at No. 10 Downing Street, a few weeks after resigning his premiership due to ill health. His legacy lies in preparing the way for the great Liberal reforms achieved by the following governments of fellow Liberals Herbert Asquith and David Lloyd George.

Campbell-Bannerman, nicknamed 'CB', was born in Glasgow, Scotland, the son of Sir James and Janet (*née* Bannerman) Campbell. He was educated at Glasgow University and Trinity College, Cambridge. Entering Parliament in 1868 as a Liberal, he abandoned his father's Tory politics. He married Charlotte Bruce in 1860. She was frequently ill and they had no children.

CB led in the manner of the consummate quiet manager, which makes sense having come from a successful business background. Acknowledged as friendly and open, he was always considered to be accessible. Following William Gladstone's retirement and Rosebery's resignation, the leadership of the Liberal Party fell to Campbell-Bannerman. He had scored high marks in his condemnation of the South African Boer War, and he seemed above and removed from the bitter Liberal Party infighting between rivals Rosebery and William Harcourt. CB therefore became the popular choice in 1899 to lead the party, and in the general election of 1906 the Liberals won a resounding victory that swept Balfour and the Conservatives out of office.

The ending of the Boer War allowed CB to quickly arrange self-government for the Union of South Africa. He aggressively sought Home Rule for Ireland and Scotland, a policy of free trade, and reform of the House of Lords. Of enormous consequence for the future, his Foreign Secretary, Sir Edward Grey, was finalising the Triple Entente treaty with France and Russia. This alliance, coupled with Britain's promise to support Belgium in the event of German invasion, would later combine to propel Britain into the catastrophe of the First World War.

Campbell-Bannerman's deteriorating health would force his early resignation, postponing many of the Liberal Party's highly anticipated social reforms until Herbert Asquith took up the reins of power. CB's wife had died in 1907, the same year that he suffered two heart attacks. He never regained his health after these events, dying in 1908 shortly after resigning from office. He is buried in the churchyard of Meigle parish church, Perthshire, Scotland.

Edward VII (reigned 1901–11) and Queen Alexandra. As King, Edward was served by four Prime Ministers: Salisbury, Balfour, Campbell-Bannerman and Asquith.

HERBERT ASQUITH

Born: 12 September 1852
Died: 15 February 1928
Party: Liberal
Served: 7 April 1908 – 7 December 1916
(8 years, 244 days)

*"Youth would be an ideal state if it
came a little later in life"*

HERBERT HENRY ASQUITH was Prime Minister for the Liberal Party in the early twentieth century. Sweeping social and political reform, along with Britain's entry into the First World War, would be his legacy. On a humanitarian level, his programme of social reforms ushered in a new era of progressive public conscience. On a political level, his government's passing of the Parliament Act (1911) brought a permanent end to the reform-blocking power of the House of Lords, definitively asserting the primacy of the House of Commons.

Asquith served more than eight continuous years as PM, demonstrating skill and self-confidence in his control of party and government. But the First World War would cast a pall over his premiership on both a political and personal level. His War Cabinet would be found wanting in the pursuit of a winning strategy, his government would be accused of failing to provide adequate munitions for the British Army on the Western Front, and the costly disaster at Gallipoli would lead to resignations and recriminations.

Devastated by the death of his son in the war, Asquith would plunge into depression and heavy abuse of alcohol to the point of being intoxicated during debate. His downward personal and political spiral would drive him out of office and his once seemingly assured political power would be diminished by the strain of waging a 'world war' whose scope he failed to completely grasp. Furthermore, he lacked the direction, energy and emotional stamina for such a colossal task. Lacking a majority in Parliament, Asquith resigned in 1916 under pressure from his own Cabinet colleagues. A coalition government led by the ambitious and energetic Secretary of War, David

Lloyd George, was formed to organise a renewed and determined effort to win the war. Asquith was shunted completely out of the government as Lloyd George assumed the wartime premiership. When Lloyd George's coalition won an overwhelming victory in the general election of 1918, it marked not only the downfall of Asquith, but also the decline of the Liberal Party.

Herbert Henry Asquith was born in Morley, Yorkshire, in 1852, the second son of Joseph and Emily (*née* Willans) Asquith. His father, a wool spinner and weaver, died when he was eight years old. Asquith was sent to live with relatives in London and won a scholarship to Oxford. He became a lawyer and in 1877 married Helen Melland, fathering four sons and one daughter. His wife died in 1891, leading to Asquith's second marriage, to Margot Tennant. By then Asquith had determined to enter politics, becoming a Liberal Party MP in 1886.

He served under Prime Minister William Gladstone as Home Secretary and under Henry Campbell-Bannerman as Chancellor of the Exchequer. Working closely with Campbell-Bannerman, Asquith and the Liberals began mapping out plans for ambitious reforms that Asquith would seek to enact during his own premiership, following his predecessor's resignation due to ill health. These reforms would include: legislation to provide pension benefits (1908) for old age retirees; the National Insurance Act (1911) to provide health insurance for those on low incomes; and blueprints for the future to help remedy poverty and protect the needy.

Asquith led the Liberals to general election victory in both January and December 1910, seeking and gaining a mandate for a progressive 'People's Budget' that the House of Lords sought desperately to block, hence the need for a Parliament Act to remove the effective veto power of the Upper Chamber. Having succeeded in this endeavour, Asquith was attempting to deal with the still thorny issue of Irish Home Rule when the First World War broke out. The Great War, as it came to be known, was to wreck and reconfigure all of Europe, and also proceeded to break Asquith and destroy much of his reputation.

He remained in the Commons until 1924, quarrelling with his former ally Lloyd George and futilely leading what was left of the war-ruined Liberal Party. He accepted a title as Earl of Oxford in 1925. Asquith died in 1928 and was buried in the churchyard of All Saints church, Sutton Courtney, Oxfordshire.

DAVID LLOYD GEORGE

Born: 17 January 1863
Died: 26 March 1945
Party: Liberal
Served: 7 December 1916 – 19 October 1922
(5 years, 317 days)

"My supreme idea is to get on. To this idea I shall sacrifice everything – except, I trust, honesty"

DAVID LLOYD GEORGE served as Prime Minister of the United Kingdom during and after the First World War by leading a coalition government consisting of disenchanted ministers who had induced Herbert Asquith's resignation. This action was prompted by a desire to pursue a more united and vigorous war effort against Germany, something that was deemed to be lacking under Asquith's ineffective leadership.

Serving under two Liberal Prime Ministers in various government capacities from 1905 to 1916, Lloyd George participated in overseeing some of the most significant Acts of Parliament since the Great Reform Act of 1832. He helped steer through Parliament Asquith's 1908 pension plan for the elderly and the 1911 National Insurance Act. Lloyd George also oversaw the passage of the Parliament Act, which blunted the power of the House of Lords to veto laws passed in the Commons. As Prime Minister from 1916, Lloyd George directed Britain's contribution to the Allies' victory in the First World War. He was a major participant in the post-war peace conference that concluded the Treaty of Versailles in 1919; and in 1921 he helped bring about the long sought after birth of the Irish Free State, thus ending decades of debate and failed attempts to reach a solution to a seemingly insoluble problem.

David Lloyd George was born in Chorlton-on-Medlock near Manchester, though his family moved almost immediately to Wales, the ancestral home of his parents. He was the eldest son of William and Elizabeth (*née* Lloyd) George, although his father died within a year of his birth and much of his upbringing was overseen by his mother's brother, Richard Lloyd. His uncle greatly influenced Lloyd George's Liberal politics and encouraged him to pursue a career in the law. After attending local Welsh schools,

Lloyd George qualified and began practising law, entering the House of Commons in 1890 as the Liberal MP for the Welsh constituency of Carnarvon. In 1888 he married Margaret Owen and they had two sons and three daughters. Following her death in 1941, he married his long-time mistress and secretary, Frances Stevenson.

In Parliament, Lloyd George gained a reputation as a Liberal reformer and outspoken champion of Welsh self-government. He gained national attention as a vocal opponent of the Boer War in South Africa (1899–1902). He was appointed President of the Board of Trade by Henry Campbell-Bannerman in 1906 and became Chancellor of the Exchequer under Herbert Asquith in 1908. Under Asquith, Lloyd George played a key role in the Liberal Party's social and parliamentary reforms then being enacted.

When the First World War broke out, many Liberals opposed British entry, but Lloyd George aggressively pursued the war effort as Minister of Munitions and later as Secretary for War. To broaden national support in order to more effectively wage the war, Asquith sought a coalition government. When this coalition Cabinet lost faith in Asquith's management of the war, Lloyd George emerged as the new Prime Minister. Lloyd George's potent and determined war leadership won this coalition government a large majority in the 1918 general election.

He then rode the crest of this victory until 1922, when the Conservatives withdrew their support and the coalition collapsed. By then, Lloyd George had represented the United Kingdom at the Versailles Conference and had achieved the compromise settlement in Ireland. The damage to the Liberal Party, however, had been significant; Asquith, Lloyd George, and the Liberals were decisively defeated in the 1924 general election and never again regained their political stature.

Lloyd George became leader of an increasingly weakened Liberal Party from 1926 to 1931, was Father of the House from 1929 to 1945, and continued to sit in the Commons until his retirement in 1945, by which time he was something of a marginal figure and relic of the past. He was ennobled in 1945 as Earl Lloyd-George of Dwyfor. He died the same year and is buried on a bluff overlooking the River Dwyfor, Ty Newydd, Llanystumdwy, Wales.

A *Punch* cartoon from April 1919 entitled 'The Easter Offering'. Lloyd George is shown presenting draft peace terms to the British people as part of finalising the Treaty of Versailles: 'I don't say it's a perfect egg, but parts of it, as the saying is, are excellent.'

ANDREW BONAR LAW

Born: 16 September 1858
Died: 30 October 1923
Party: Conservative
Served: 23 October 1922 – 20 May 1923
             (209 days)

*"If I am a great man,
then a good many great men of
history are frauds"*

ANDREW BONAR LAW was the first, and only, Prime Minister to be born outside the British Isles. Born in Kingston (Rexton), colonial New Brunswick, in what today is Canada, he was the son of James Law, a Presbyterian minister, and his wife Elizabeth (*née* Kidston). His mother died when he was only three years old, and Andrew (referred to as Bonar) then moved to Scotland to live with his mother's sister. He was thereafter raised and schooled in Scotland. Thanks to his superior intellect in school, his outstanding gift for business, and his relatives' financial support, Bonar Law gained a position in the Jacks Ironworks Company. This business, coupled with a family inheritance, brought Bonar Law the necessary wealth to enter politics.

His politics can be summed up in the two issues he opposed: Free Trade and Irish Home Rule. He led the Conservative Party in its fight for tariff reform, which meant 'limited' tariffs on imports and rejection of free trade. And he contested the Liberal Party's attempts to bring about Irish Home Rule prior to the First World War.

He married Annie Pitcairn Robley in 1891 and raised eight children, including two sons who were killed in the First World War. His wife died young, in 1909, and Bonar Law never remarried. Serving under George V from late 1922 to early 1923, his term of office lasted barely more than 200 days. Serious ill health in the form of cancer forced his resignation in May 1923 and he died the following October.

Bonar Law was acknowledged as an articulate speaker, a pragmatic politician, and a man who could get along and work with both sides of the parliamentary divide.

A teetotaller known for his fine chess playing, Bonar Law was the polar opposite of numerous grandees who had preceded him in the top job – Prime Ministers of leisure, music, art, and horse-racing, of manor houses and shared 'old boy' school and university experiences. Herbert Asquith called him 'the unknown Prime Minister'. He is buried in Westminster Abbey.

George V (reigned 1911–36). He was served by five Prime Ministers: Asquith, Lloyd George, Bonar Law, Baldwin and Ramsay MacDonald.

STANLEY BALDWIN

Born:	3 August 1867
Died:	14 December 1947
Party:	Conservative
Served:	23 May 1923 – 16 January 1924
	4 November 1924 – 5 June 1929
	7 June 1935 – 28 May 1937
	(7 years and 82 days)

*"I would rather be an opportunist
and float than go to the bottom
with my principles round my neck"*

STANLEY BALDWIN was three-time Prime Minister of the United Kingdom, serving under three different monarchs: George V, Edward VIII (albeit briefly), and George VI. His three terms encompassed the difficult period following the First World War with its suffocating war debts and labour turmoil, the depths of the global Great Depression, and the threatening emergence of Hitler and the Nazis during the 1930s. The challenges of these multiple crises, all coming on top of each other, would have taxed the abilities of any leader of any period in history. As it was, though, Baldwin and his Labour counterpart Ramsay MacDonald struggled mightily with these events while playing leapfrog with the premiership from 1923 until Baldwin's retirement in 1937.

Industrial, financial, and economic upheaval provided the background that encouraged a policy of diplomatic appeasement to Hitler. Avoidance of another major military conflict was the paramount objective in order to avoid the staggering cost of potential human suffering and the actual expense of increased military preparedness. At that time, the reluctance to challenge Hitler seemed prudent to most, but has since given critics the ammunition to lay great blame at the feet of the interwar Prime Ministers. It should be remembered that MacDonald, Baldwin, and Neville Chamberlain suffered continuous criticism at the time, for both their domestic and foreign policies, and it is debatable whether anyone else could have truly altered the course of events.

Baldwin was born in Bewdley, Worcestershire, the only son of Alfred and Louisa (*née* MacDonald) Baldwin. He was educated at Harrow and Cambridge, and did not enter Parliament until 1908 at the age of forty-one, being instead involved in the running of his wealthy father's iron and steel companies. His fortune was considerable, so much so that in 1919 Baldwin personally donated £150,000 to the Treasury in order help pay off war debts.

Baldwin entered the Cabinet of Prime Minister David Lloyd George in 1921, as President of the Board of Trade, having previously served as Financial Secretary between 1917 and 1921. Baldwin and Andrew Bonar Law then led an effort to oust Lloyd George, whom Baldwin felt was corrupt and out of step in his policies. This resulted in a Conservative Party victory in the general election of 1922 and the elevation of Bonar Law to Prime Minister with Baldwin serving as Chancellor of the Exchequer. Shortly thereafter, when Bonar Law became critically ill with cancer and was forced to resign, Baldwin assumed the post of Prime Minister. It was his ability to lead, maintain and control the Conservative Party during the 1920s that deflected a potentially more radical shift to a socialist government. His political dexterity in isolating the Liberals under Lloyd George, while including Labour's Ramsay MacDonald in the National Coalition government, allowed the Conservatives to emerge as a viable and formidable alternative to radical change.

Baldwin, in his first two terms during the 1920s, dealt with high unemployment and domestic labour strife, while also seeking disarmament agreements with fellow European powers in order to stave off another catastrophic war. In 1935 he took over from an exhausted Ramsay MacDonald, his coalition government seeking to control German and Italian aggression through the collective efforts of the Great Powers in concert with the increasingly impotent League of Nations. Proposals were now put forward to begin modestly, and belatedly, rearming Britain for a possible conflict with Hitler. Baldwin planned on retiring upon Edward VIII's coronation, but that too came apart in scandal and constitutional controversy when Edward insisted on marrying American divorcee Mrs Wallis Simpson, forcing his abdication. George VI's coronation in 1936 then became Baldwin's curtain call as he retired the following year.

He married Lucy Risdale in 1892, and they had four sons and three daughters. Retiring from the Commons in 1937, he was created the 1st Earl of Bewdley. His reputation suffered dramatically with the onset of the Second World War, as he received increasing blame for inaction in the face of Hitler's aggression. Yet the following decades have partly tempered that judgement. Baldwin died in 1947, was cremated, and his remains are buried in Worcester Cathedral in the county of his birth.

JAMES RAMSAY MACDONALD

Born:	12 October 1866
Died:	9 November 1937
Party:	Labour
Served:	22 January 1924 – 4 November 1924
	5 June 1929 – 7 June 1935
	(6 years, 289 days)

"We hear war called murder.
It is not: it is suicide"

JAMES RAMSAY MACDONALD was the first Labour Party Prime Minister, taking office in 1924 and again in 1929. Ironically, the Labour Party would later expel MacDonald for his formation of a coalition National Government to lead Britain during the crises of the Great Depression and the rise of Hitler in Europe during the early 1930s. This alleged betrayal by MacDonald of the principles of the Labour movement obscures the significance of his achievements. He gave Labour its first experience of government, thereby bringing the party into the mainstream of British politics.

Ramsay MacDonald came from humble origins, being born in Lossiemouth, Scotland, to farm labourer James MacDonald and housemaid Anne Ramsay. MacDonald was educated at the local parish schools and later studied numerous subjects at the Birkbeck Literary and Scientific Institution. He married Margaret Ethel Gladstone (no relation to PM William Gladstone) in 1896. She died in 1911, shortly after giving birth to their sixth child. Her death devastated MacDonald, and he never fully recovered.

MacDonald made his early living in London as a journalist pursuing socialist ideals and politics. His marriage to the daughter of the distinguished scientist Dr John Hall Gladstone brought him some financial independence and he entered Parliament in 1906. By 1911 MacDonald had become leader of the small but growing Labour Party, which agreed to support Herbert Asquith's Liberal Party in return for not being challenged in certain parliamentary constituencies. MacDonald bitterly opposed Britain's entry into the First World War in 1914, seeking a negotiated peace instead. However, the Labour Party split over the issue, and MacDonald lost his seat in Parliament.

By 1922 MacDonald had regained his seat and the leadership of Labour Party, which now eclipsed the Liberals and became the leading opposition to the Conservatives. Through his persuasion, Labour had refused to join the Communist International, keeping them within the relative mainstream of British politics, although they were still viewed as dangerous socialists by those on the political right. The decline of, and incessant infighting among, the Liberals provided an opening for Labour, and in 1924 MacDonald became the first Labour Prime Minister.

He chose to be his own Foreign Secretary and concentrated on foreign affairs. Some minor social reforms were achieved in the Housing and Coal Mine Acts, but no major or radical reforms were attempted as MacDonald sought to demonstrate that the Labour Party could responsibly run the country. MacDonald lasted less than a year in office before being replaced by Conservative Stanley Baldwin, who had also preceded him. Baldwin held the premiership until the 1929 election put MacDonald and Labour back into power, albeit in a minority government.

By now MacDonald was faced with the onerous task of leading Britain through the Great Depression of the early 1930s, sky-high unemployment, and the rise of Hitler's Nazi Germany. In order to remain in office and provide a desperately needed united effort to confront the economic crisis, MacDonald agreed to lead a coalition government in 1931 supported by Liberals and Conservatives. Because this government was predominantly Conservative, MacDonald earned the label of 'traitor' and 'betrayer' from the Labour Party and its followers. When the coalition won the general election of 1931, it only increased the bitterness that 'true' Labourites felt for their former hero.

While Britain remained in the grip of economic chaos and facing the re-emergence of a German threat rapidly growing from 1933, MacDonald's health began to fail. Disowned by his former party and friends, and overwhelmed by national and international problems, he agreed to resign in 1935, returning the premiership to Stanley Baldwin.

After losing his seat in Parliament in 1935, MacDonald managed to return in 1936, but by now his health and energy were spent. He embarked on a cruise to South America to help in his convalescence, but he died at sea in November 1937. Returned to Britain, he was buried beside his wife in the 'Old Spynie' churchyard, outside Lossiemouth.

NEVILLE CHAMBERLAIN

Born:	18 March 1869
Died:	9 November 1940
Party:	Conservative
Served:	28 May 1937 – 10 May 1940
	(2 years, 348 days)

"Peace with honour …
Peace for our time"
(on the Munich Agreement)

NEVILLE CHAMBERLAIN will be forever remembered as the Prime Minister who signed the infamous Munich Agreement with Adolf Hitler in 1938. This was to be the conclusive act of Chamberlain's policy of appeasement toward Hitler and the Nazis. Instead of securing, in Chamberlain's words, 'peace in our time' and the avoidance of another world war, it encouraged Hitler to pursue his power-hungry plans and set in motion the events that led to the outbreak of the Second World War.

Neville Chamberlain was the second son born to political heavyweight Joseph Chamberlain. His mother, Florence Kenrick, was Joseph Chamberlain's second wife and died when Neville was only six. His older half-brother Austen was raised for a political career and became a leading Conservative politician. Neville's upbringing was geared toward future management of the family business interests. His schooling was at Rugby, and then at Mason College (now Birmingham University). He worked in the Bahamas from 1890 to 1897, returning to England to conduct business and enter local government in Birmingham. In 1911 he married Anne Vere Cole, raising one son and one daughter.

Chamberlain worked his way from local to national politics, entering Parliament in 1918. A series of positions in the Conservative governments of Andrew Bonar Law and Stanley Baldwin brought Chamberlain to national prominence. He was particularly successful as Minister of Health (1923, 1924–29, and 1931). As Chancellor of the Exchequer (1923–24 and 1931–37) Chamberlain practised a fiscal policy that refused to promote the massive expenditure for military rearmament that many felt was necessary to prepare for the threats posed by Nazi Germany and Fascist Italy. This in turn led to his faith in the need to negotiate and, if necessary, to appease the European dictators in order to avoid another world war that Chamberlain feared could not be afforded or won. This was the route he chose from 1937 when he became Prime Minister upon the retirement of the seventy-year-old Stanley Baldwin.

Upon his return from the Munich Conference in September 1938, Chamberlain was hailed as a hero and saviour; only a few strident anti-appeasement naysayers, led by Winston Churchill and his handful of fringe politicians, condemned the agreement. Nearly everyone else, from the mainstream press to the general public and a majority in Parliament, backed the agreement in the belief that another European war had been averted. Almost everyone expected Hitler and Germany to do the rational thing and accept the territorial concession of the Sudetenland in Czechoslovakia, bring to an end any further foreign policy ambitions and thereby avoid unnecessary war. Almost everyone was soon shown to be completely wrong.

When, in March 1939, Germany invaded and devoured the rest of Czechoslovakia, the worthlessness of Hitler's word and the Munich Agreement became clear, and the inevitability of war became all too apparent. Rearmament, already in progress to some extent, became the foremost priority. A promise by Britain and France to defend Poland, Hitler's next target, was then concluded. A belated offer to include the Soviet Union in a defence agreement against Nazi Germany was attempted but rebuffed. Instead, to everyone's surprise, Germany and the USSR signed a Non-Aggression Pact in August 1939. Within the month Poland was invaded and Britain was at war.

Chamberlain's policy was revealed as not only failing to prevent war, but was now viewed as having been an encouragement to the European dictators to conquer and carve up Europe as they saw fit. Chamberlain has been castigated ever since, and a further charge – also levelled at his predecessors MacDonald and Baldwin – is that Chamberlain also failed to adequately rearm Britain in the face of what appeared to some to be inevitable and imminent war. These are serious accusations, and decades later Chamberlain continues to be popularly blamed as a foolish appeaser, although some historians have attempted to reassess his premiership and restore his reputation.

A crushed Chamberlain held on to his position until the following spring, but it was evident that he was not the man to lead the nation through a major war. The disaster of the Norwegian campaign in the spring of 1940 led to his resignation and the selection of the most vocal of the anti-appeasement prophets, Winston Churchill, to replace him.

Broken in spirit and suffering from a rapid deterioration of health, Neville Chamberlain died in November 1940 and is buried in Westminster Abbey.

WINSTON CHURCHILL

Born:	30 November 1874
Died:	24 January 1965
Party:	Conservative
Served:	10 May 1940 – 26 July 1945
	26 October 1951 – 7 April 1955
	(8 years, 240 days)

"Those who can win a war well can rarely make a good peace, and those who could make a good peace would never have won the war"

WINSTON CHURCHILL, twice Prime Minister of the United Kingdom, holds for many a special place in the pantheon of history's great men. A man of enormous talent, energy, and accomplishment, he led Britain – and for a time the free world – in one of its gravest and darkest hours. Besides his strong leadership during the Second World War, Churchill strode the world stage for over half a century, playing a major role in many of Britain's, and the world's, defining events. Routinely outrageous in his actions and controversial in his opinions, he exhibited an enthusiasm for action that frightened some, appalled others, and frequently baffled even his most admiring supporters. He was a man of incredible curiosity that often led to endless meddling. He possessed gargantuan appetites for food and drink, and his output of oratory and prose was prodigious. He revelled in sampling the world for its experiences, contacts, and pleasures. He lived life to the fullest in all phases of his existence, though he suffered from bouts of depression that he characterised as his 'black dog' days.

Churchill was born at Blenheim Palace, ancestral home of John Churchill, the 1st Duke of Marlborough and Churchill's greatly admired military forebear. His father was Lord Randolph Churchill, brother of the 8th Duke and a formidable politician in his own right. His mother was a wealthy American, Jennie Jerome. Churchill was educated at Harrow and the Royal Military College at Sandhurst. He was an indifferent student but a voracious reader. He received a commission in the 4th Queen's Own Hussars and his early career involved military assignments in such far-flung outposts of the British Empire as India and Africa. He participated in one of the world's last great cavalry charges at the Battle of Omdurman in the Sudan.

Resigning from the military, Churchill served as a war correspondent in the South African Boer War. Captured as a prisoner of war, he made an amazing escape that he chronicled to great acclaim and fame. Entering Parliament in 1895, Churchill began his political career as a Conservative, but was to switch back and forth between the Liberal and Conservative parties. He was always considered a maverick for his unpredictability and his quixotic views and positions.

The First World War found Churchill as First Lord of the Admiralty under Herbert Asquith's Liberal government. Churchill's plan to knock Turkey out of the war and open another front inspired the Gallipoli invasion, a disaster of tragically huge proportions that caused him to resign. It remained a stain on his reputation for the rest of his life. Leaving England and Parliament, Churchill went to France and rejoined his old regiment, serving for several months in the trenches on the Western Front. He finished the war serving as Minister of Munitions under Prime Minister David Lloyd George.

The years between the world wars saw Churchill's career fall from the heights of government to the depths of virtual obscurity, and then rise again to prominence. His willingness to send a military mission to Russia in an attempt to crush the Bolsheviks in the Russian Civil War, along with his bellicose response to strikers during the labour turmoil of the 1920s, made him a consistent enemy of the Labour Party. He served in several government positions during the 1920s, including Secretary of War and Chancellor of the Exchequer, but the 1930s saw him exiled and overlooked. Particularly ignored were his trenchant and persistent warnings of the looming threat of Hitler and Nazi Germany. He consistently encouraged Britain to rearm in the face of Nazi aggression in Europe and endlessly denounced the policy of appeasement as caving in to Hitler's insatiable demands while allowing Germany to bulk up its military muscle. By 1939 and the German invasion of Poland it became apparent to all that Churchill had been right. He returned to government, initially as First Lord of the Admiralty (the post he had vacated in disgrace during the last war), and then as Prime Minister following the resignation of the demoralised Neville Chamberlain.

The Second World War would become Churchill's 'finest hour'. After the fall of France in 1940, Britain stood alone and isolated, but the nation was buoyed by Churchill's inspirational courage and commitment to never surrender. Although he abhorred and feared Soviet Russia, he desperately required her help against the common enemy, and he nurtured and maintained a military alliance with Stalin out of necessity for the duration of the war. Despite some notable tactical mistakes, such as early on in the war sending a pair of lightly escorted warships (*Repulse* and *Prince of Wales*) to their watery graves at the hands of Japanese warplanes, Churchill was an effective leader and possessed the energy and determination to persevere even when victory seemed all too distant.

To his surprise and disappointment, Churchill would be defeated in the general election in 1945 that followed the conclusion of the war. Clement Attlee and the Labour Party would come to power, and Churchill would again be turned out of office. He then directed his attention to the Cold War threat of the Soviet Union. In a famous 1946 speech, Churchill would coin the phrase 'Iron Curtain' to describe the divide in Europe between the communist east from the democratic west. Vindication would again be Churchill's reward, as he was returned to office as Prime Minister in the 1951 general election. But clearly he was a man whose health and age were working against him. He had endured a heart attack during the Second World War, and in his mid-seventies he suffered a stroke. He soldiered on until 1955, when at the age of eighty-one he retired, handing over the premiership to Sir Anthony Eden, his Foreign Secretary.

In his private life, Churchill married Clementine Hozier in 1908 and they had one son and four daughters. Elsewhere, his writing career was a success of enormous magnitude, bringing fame and reward. His four-volume *History of the English-Speaking Peoples* and *The Second World War*, his mammoth six-volume history of the conflict, would earn him the Noble Prize for Literature in 1953. Furthermore, he was an accomplished bricklayer and artist, painting being a lifelong passion that brought him great relaxation wherever and whenever he travelled.

Churchill was made Knight of the Garter in 1953 but declined a peerage, declaring that he desired to be buried a commoner, even though he was anything but common. When he did die, in London in 1965, he was honoured with a magnificent state funeral in St Paul's Cathedral. He is buried in the graveyard of St Martin's church, Bladon, Oxfordshire. Churchill's manor house, Chartwell in Kent, is today open to the public. The brick wall that he patiently built while enduring his 1930s exile from government can be viewed there. Upon his death in 1965, Churchill was the first statesman to lie in state in Westminster Hall since William Gladstone. Big Ben was held silent from morning until midnight as the world mourned one of the true titans of the twentieth century.

The 'Big Three' at the Yalta Conference in 1945: Winston Churchill (left),
Franklin Roosevelt (centre), and Josef Stalin (right).

CLEMENT ATTLEE

Born:	3 January 1883
Died:	8 October 1967
Party:	Labour
Served:	26 July 1945 – 26 October 1951
	(6 years, 92 days)

"Often the experts make the worst possible ministers in their own fields. In this country we prefer rule by amateurs"

CLEMENT ATTLEE served as Prime Minister from 1945 to 1951, leading a Labour government under King George VI. During this post-war period, the United Kingdom was completely transformed by breathtaking social reforms and the radical nationalisation of major British industries. The dramatic depth and range of these changes, combined with the swiftness of their implementation, was unprecedented in modern British history.

Britain had been nearly bankrupted and broken by the enormous cost and energy necessary to win two world wars within a thirty-year period. Though grateful for Churchill's leadership in waging the Second World War, the British people were now ready for domestic change; the general election of summer 1945 would reveal the mood of the nation. Labour won a landslide victory and swept the Tories out of office. Clement Attlee and his party set about establishing a welfare state that included a National Health Service and reforms in the areas of education, employment and social security, among others.

The groundwork for these reforms had been developed in the preceding years, not least in the Beveridge Report (1942) which identified and sought to solve five 'Giant Evils' in society: squalor, ignorance, want, idleness and disease. After 1945, the Labour-controlled Parliament could now implement many of the proposed solutions, which became widely accepted and approved as a social safety net for all citizens; they remain largely in place, though modified, to this day.

Attlee's government did not stop there. Policies and planning inspired by socialist thought were implemented to manage the economy, set wages, standardise working conditions, and fully empower trade unions in the management of business and industry. These ambitious policies – contested by the Conservatives and largely undone by Margaret Thatcher decades later – included the nationalisation of such industries as coal, steel, railways, communication, and mining.

So who was Clement Attlee, and how was he able to achieve this extraordinary seismic shift in the British political and economic landscape? Attlee was born in January 1883, the son of Henry Attlee and Harriet Watson, in Putney, London. His father was a successful solicitor and his upbringing was middle-class. His education at University College, Oxford, trained him for a career in law, but his dedicated social work in the East End of London acquainted him with the realities of poverty and the disaffected, leading Attlee to become a socialist.

During the First World War, Attlee's political affiliation to the anti-war Independent Labour Party did not prevent him from volunteering for the military, serving on several fronts and rising to the rank of major. Returning to London's East End and entering politics, Attlee was soon a Member of Parliament, representing Limehouse. As a Labour MP, he drew attention for his competency and rose quickly in Ramsay MacDonald's Labour government of the mid-1920s, eventually serving as Under-Secretary of War.

Attlee gained a reputation for being quietly efficient and able to get things done. He also was careful about staking out his own political course. In the 1930s, he deftly dodged taking sides with either the pro-communist elements of the Labour Party or its anti-rearmament wing. This enhanced Attlee's credibility to such an extent that during the Second World War, in Winston Churchill's coalition government, Attlee held numerous ministerial posts, not the least of which was Deputy Prime Minister. While Churchill ran the war and masterminded foreign affairs, Attlee handled domestic matters. Attlee also chaired Cabinet meetings during Churchill's frequent wartime trips abroad. As the war neared its conclusion, Attlee maintained Labour Party discipline, strengthened his leadership position, and led the Labour Party to its dramatic and startling victory over Churchill and the Conservatives. He immediately set to work revolutionising Britain's social commitment and responsibilities, as promised to constituents, and coupled these changes to the economic and industrial transformation of ownership and operation. It was a makeover of bewildering proportions.

Attlee did not ignore foreign affairs. He hastened the British withdrawal from India and the creation of an independent India and Pakistan in 1947; he pulled Britain out of Palestine as the state of Israel was being born (as envisaged by the Balfour Declaration); he withdrew Britain from Ceylon and Burma; and in the face of potential Soviet aggression Attlee fully committed to the North Atlantic Treaty Organization (NATO) with the United States. To the chagrin of many Labourites of more pacifist persuasion, he also sought to maintain a strong military with nuclear capabilities.

After six years in power marked by such comprehensive change, Attlee and the Labour Party's agenda ran out of steam. A multitude of economic problems brought on by the Second World War caught up with Britain and Europe as a whole. Churchill and the Conservatives regained power in 1951, and Attlee was relegated to leading the opposition for the next four years. He retired in 1955, at the age of seventy-two, accepting an earldom that made him the 1st Earl Attlee. He died in 1967 and is buried in Westminster Abbey.

Though never possessing the larger than life personality of a Churchill, the diffident Attlee was nevertheless able to adroitly manoeuvre himself and Labour into a position that brought about revolutionary social and economic change. This socially responsible role of government has become the accepted and expected standard in British life. Attlee was able to successfully bridge the divergent wings of his party, ensuring the necessary support to push through his programme of reform. This is the truest test of any leader in politics. Moreover, Attlee was no shrinking violet when it came to exercising the prerogatives of a Prime Minister: he could wield the axe when subordinates were not fulfilling expectations. Few PMs have dismissed as many ministers and underlings as Attlee, using a legendary abruptness to remove those whose performance was deemed unsatisfactory. Beneath the facade of a quiet, pipe-smoking, cricket-loving, middle-class everyman was a ruthless politician of enormous imagination, intelligence and skill. Clement Attlee summed up his career in a frequently quoted limerick of his own writing:

> *Few thought he was even a starter*
> *There were many who thought themselves smarter*
> *But he ended up PM*
> *CH and OM*
> *An earl and knight of the garter.*

Attlee at work in Number 10 Downing Street.

SIR ANTHONY EDEN

Born: 12 June 1897
Died: 14 January 1977
Party: Conservative
Served: 7 April 1955 – 10 January 1957
(1 year, 279 days)

"If you've broken the eggs,
you should make the omelette"

SERVING THREE TIMES as Foreign Secretary, notably during the Second World War, Anthony Eden's career forte was foreign affairs. Yet as Prime Minister it was a foreign policy disaster involving the Suez Canal that embarrassed his government and brought about his resignation.

Anthony Eden did not lack for experience, either practical or intellectual. The son of Sir William Eden and Sybil Grey, Eden attended Eton and Oxford, graduating with honours in Oriental languages. He served on the Western Front during the First World War, advancing in rank to become a brigade major and being decorated with the Military Cross for bravery. Two of his brothers were killed in this world war; his son would be killed in the next. His mother was a descendant of Charles Grey, the Prime Minister who oversaw the passage of the Great Reform Bill in 1832. Anthony opted for a career in politics and was elected in 1923 to the House of Commons, where he would remain until his resignation in 1957.

In 1935 he was appointed by Stanley Baldwin to be Foreign Secretary. Three years later he resigned this position in protest due to then PM Neville Chamberlain's willingness to deal with Italy's dictator Benito Mussolini. This action won Eden a great deal of admiration from anti-appeasement politicians such as Winston Churchill. When war broke out and Churchill became Prime Minister, it was Eden he favoured with the position of Foreign Secretary. Eden served with distinction during the war and was appointed again when Churchill regained office in 1951. It was assumed by many that when Churchill decided to step down Eden would replace him. In April 1955, due to Churchill's advanced age and ill health, this came to pass.

For that matter, Eden's health was not good either. He had undergone three major operations in 1953, leaving him with frequent high fevers. His reputation for being hot-tempered did not help his relations with either his Cabinet or the press. But his outward public persona tended to be suave and charming. He struggled, however, with domestic issues, as his background had always been foreign affairs. He called an immediate election in 1955, won a majority, and seemed on track for success.

Yet in July 1956 Egyptian leader Gamal Abdel Nasser, who had pro-Soviet leanings, nationalised the Suez Canal. Eden felt the time had come to reassert Britain's power on the world stage to prevent the loss of control over this vital waterway. Previously, as Foreign Secretary, Eden had negotiated the withdrawal of British forces from the Canal Zone on an American guarantee of international access, which was now being threatened. Acting in concert with France and Israel, Britain invaded Egypt and seized the Canal. Eden was stunned by the storm of protest that followed. The demand for immediate withdrawal came from Egypt and her fellow Middle-Eastern Arab nations, heavily backed by both the Soviet Union and the United Nations. Intense pressure to withdraw was also applied by Britain's erstwhile ally the United States, which fully supported the UN and Egypt. Eden was forced to capitulate, leaving the former 'Great Power' publicly humbled on the world stage. A politically humiliated Eden took leave to Jamaica to recover his declining physical health, and upon his return he resigned his position in January 1957.

He also left the Commons in 1957 and never returned to politics, remaining unwell for the rest of his life. He had married Beatrice Beckett in 1923; they had three children (one dying in infancy) but were divorced in 1950. In 1952 he married Clarissa Churchill, niece of Winston Churchill. Eden was created Earl of Avon in 1961 and died in 1977. He is buried in St Mary's churchyard, Alvediston, Wiltshire.

Eden (far right) as Foreign Secretary during Churchill's second premiership. They are pictured at the White House, meeting their American counterparts: Secretary of State John Foster Dulles (far left) and President Dwight D. Eisenhower. These cordial relations would be damaged by the Suez Crisis during Eden's own premiership.

HAROLD MACMILLAN

Born: 10 February 1894
Died: 29 December 1986
Party: Conservative
Served: 10 January 1957 – 18 October 1963
(6 years, 281 days)

"A man who trusts nobody is apt to be the kind of man no one trusts"

HAROLD MACMILLAN became Prime Minister of the United Kingdom upon the resignation of Sir Anthony Eden following the Suez Crisis. Macmillan rescued the Conservative Party, and the reputation of the UK, from this humiliation with the pursuit of growth in Britain's mixed economy and strong resistance to Soviet Communism and influence. A fortunate wave of prosperity in the late 1950s, and his memorable sound bite that Britons had 'never had it so good', brought Macmillan and the Conservatives victory in the 1959 general election and another term in office.

Macmillan sought membership of the burgeoning European Economic Community, but was flatly rejected by French President Charles de Gaulle. Earlier in the decade, Anthony Eden had dismissed an opportunity to participate in the formation of the union, but now, upon requesting membership, Britain was being rejected by the notoriously pompous de Gaulle. Macmillan instead turned his foreign policy attention west to an increased alliance with the United States and cultivation of the 'special relationship'. This renewed co-operation proved especially useful for Britain's resurgent nuclear capability, as Macmillan negotiated the purchase of the new Polaris submarine-launched missile, further underscoring his determination to restore Britain's world-power status. In turn, the US appreciated Macmillan's world-view concerning the threat of Soviet influence. His position of renewed strength would help him in the negotiations for the first Nuclear Test Ban Treaty in 1963.

Harold Macmillan was born in London in 1894, the son of Maurice and Helen (*née* Belles) Macmillan. His mother was an American and his grandfather had been the founder of the Macmillan publishing house. His privileged upbringing saw him educated at both Eton and Oxford. His university education was, however, interrupted by his enlistment in the Grenadier Guards during the First World War. He served with distinction on the Western Front and was twice wounded, once at the Battle of Loos, and again, this time severely, at the Somme. He was in hospital for two years recovering from his wounds.

In 1920 Macmillan married Lady Dorothy Cavendish, daughter of the 9th Duke of Devonshire and descendant of William Cavendish, the 4th Duke and Prime Minister from 1756 to 1757. They had one son and three daughters. Macmillan was elected to Parliament for Stockton-on-Tees in 1924. His anti-appeasement position during the 1930s, though unpopular with mainstream opinion, caught the attention of Winston Churchill and reaped rewards with the outbreak of the Second World War. Churchill's support during the war landed Macmillan several government position. He was eventually appointed as Resident Minister in North Africa, where he established a close relationship with American General (and later President) Dwight Eisenhower.

Macmillan then rose through the ranks of the Conservative Party in post-war government positions as Minister of Housing (1951–54), Minister of Defence (1954–55), Foreign Secretary (1955), and Chancellor of the Exchequer (1955–57). His rise culminated in the premiership upon the resignation of Eden in 1957. Though restoring confidence and achieving some successes, particularly in foreign affairs, Macmillan was to fall victim to a faltering economy and a sex scandal that discredited his government and contributed to his political demise. The Profumo Affair of 1963 featured a lurid mixing of sex and spies. Macmillan's Secretary of State for War, John Profumo, first lied to the Commons then admitted his affair with Christine Keeler, who also happened be having an affair with a senior Soviet naval attaché (and probable intelligence agent). The fallout from the scandal, beyond the potential security breach, nearly brought down the government and hastened Macmillan's resignation. His emergency operation for prostate cancer in October 1963 provided the cover for his exit. Before leaving office, Macmillan wielded his considerable influence in the choice of his successor, Alec Douglas-Home.

Macmillan soon retired from the Commons in 1964, recovered from his prostate cancer, published his memoirs, and accepted a title, Earl of Stockton, in 1984. He died in 1986 and is buried in the family plot of the St Giles churchyard, Horsted Keynes, West Sussex.

Macmillan with President John F. Kennedy in December 1961. They were on very good terms, despite the age difference, and agreed on much Cold War policy.

SIR ALEC DOUGLAS-HOME

Born: 2 July 1903
Died: 9 October 1995
Party: Conservative
Served: 18 October 1963 – 16 October 1964
(362 days)

"There are two problems in my life. The political ones are insoluble and the economic ones are incomprehensible"

SIR ALEC DOUGLAS-HOME was one of the more unusual Prime Ministers of the twentieth century. He was something of a throwback to the era when titled peers, born to wealth and privilege, dominated the political scene. He served in the House of Lords as the 14th Earl of Home, but he was much more than a titled peer. He was a first-class cricket player as well as a lifelong politician who willingly renounced his title in order to serve as Prime Minister under Queen Elizabeth II after the resignation of Harold Macmillan.

Douglas-Home was the eldest son of Charles Douglas, 13th Earl of Home (pronounced 'Hume') and Lady Lilian Lambton, descendant of Charles Grey, who had been the PM behind the Great Reform Act of 1832. Educated at Eton and Oxford, Douglas-Home played several years of first-class cricket at the county level and served in the House of Commons until inheriting his father's title in 1951. Upon the resignation of Harold Macmillan, the Queen invited Douglas-Home to form a government, but he thought it impractical to serve as Prime Minister from the House of Lords. He therefore used a newly passed law, the Peerage Act of 1963, to renounce his noble title and thereafter sought to re-enter the Commons, which he did after a few weeks as PM, following a by-election.

Douglas-Home had originally entered the House of Commons in 1931, but contracted tuberculosis of the spine in 1938, and was bedridden in the early 1940s. He recovered to become Commonwealth Secretary in 1955 under Anthony Eden, and Foreign Secretary in 1960 under Harold Macmillan. He was respected as an excellent administrator, a skilful negotiator, and a savvy decision-maker. His politics were conservative yet practical; he was in favour of joining the European Common Market and maintaining healthy continental ties, and he was staunch in his willingness to stand up to the Soviet Union. He surprised many with his determination to become Prime Minister and lead the Conservative Party while a member of the House of Lords, the first since Lord Salisbury sixty years earlier, though he soon disclaimed his title and won election to the Commons.

His heritage was, of course, a subject of derision and ridicule by Harold Wilson and the Labour Party. His background made him an easy and convenient target. But Douglas-Home was calm, stable, and deliberate. His Cold War policy of resisting the Soviet Union and maintaining Britain's nuclear deterrent resonated well, even in the face of the Campaign for Nuclear Disarmament that was growing in support at the time. In 1964 Douglas-Home ran an effective campaign in the general election but narrowly lost out to Wilson and Labour. He resigned as leader of the Conservatives the following year, but served under Edward Heath as Foreign Secretary (1970–74), finally retiring thereafter.

He had married Elizabeth Alington in 1936 and they had three daughters and one son. Restored to the nobility in 1974 with the title Baron Home of the Hirsel, he died in 1995 and is buried in the village cemetery at Lennel, Coldstream, in the Scottish Borders.

The Beatles in February 1964 during their bid to conquer America. Their novelty, youth and vibrancy contrasted with Britain's more traditional Tory government at the time. Douglas-Home seemed out of touch to many, while Harold Wilson successfully harnessed the mood of change, bringing thirteen years of Tory rule to an end.

HAROLD WILSON

Born: 11 March 1916
Died: 24 May 1995
Party: Labour
Served: 16 October 1964 – 19 June 1970
4 March 1974 – 5 April 1976
(7 years, 279 days)

*"I am an optimist, but an optimist
who carries a raincoat"*

Twice Prime Minister, Harold Wilson led the Labour Party to victory in four out of five general elections, then voluntarily retired while still PM in seemingly good health and at the height of his powers (although it later became known that he was beginning to suffer from early-onset Alzheimer's disease). He was known and respected for his keen intelligence, brilliant debating skill, and down-to-earth mannerisms. He was able to unite the various elements of the Labour Party, managing to prevent the more extreme elements from destroying his carefully constructed coalition of diverse factions. It was a successful recipe for keeping Wilson and Labour in power, though not necessarily a prescription for remedying the ills of Britain.

Wilson was born in Huddersfield, West Yorkshire, the son of James and Ethel (*née* Seddon) Wilson. His father was an industrial chemist and his upbringing was largely middle-class. He won a scholarship to Oxford and obtained a first-class degree in Philosophy, Politics and Economics. After lecturing at a university level, Wilson worked as a civil servant during the Second World War and in 1945 was elected to Parliament. His rise was swift, and he became President of the Board of Trade in 1947 at the age of just thirty-one.

By 1963, Wilson had become leader of the Labour Party and he went on to become Prime Minister in 1964 after a successful general election campaign. Another election victory in 1966 kept Wilson in power until 1970 when defeat to the Conservatives left him and Labour in opposition. Victory in two general elections of 1974 returned Wilson to office, but his government's parliamentary position was somewhat precarious during this time. His attempts to bring the UK into the European Common Market during the

1960s had failed, but that did not necessarily displease many of his fellow Labourites. The Conservatives under Edward Heath then finally accomplished this task, and the question now became to what degree the UK should participate.

His method for dealing with the powerful trade unions, to which the Labour Party was affiliated, was to give in to their demands over wages, rights, and influence. Beset by high inflation, unemployment, and a stagnant economy, the 1960s and 1970s saw the UK continuously plagued by economic problems. Internationally, Wilson managed to keep Britain out of the quagmire of the Vietnam War, rebuffing all American invitations to participate, but he continued the policy of 'direct rule' over Northern Ireland as Britain struggled to deal with the persistent 'Troubles'.

After emerging narrowly victorious in the general elections of 1974, Wilson found the divergent factions of the Labour Party growing further apart and more difficult to control under his pragmatic style of leadership. The 'hard Left' became disenchanted with his lack of radical enthusiasm and, conversely, Wilson began to recognise and contest their influence within the Labour movement. This was to be a theme of Wilson's politics for the rest of his life: the fear that the Labour Party would render itself irrelevant and unattractive to the electorate if it moved too far to the left and sought more radical socialist aims. Indeed, a leftward shift in the party would occur in the coming years that would keep Labour out of power until the emergence of 'New Labour' under Tony Blair and the recasting of the party's image in the mid-1990s.

In a shocking and well-kept surprise action, Wilson abruptly resigned the premiership in 1976, turning the reins over to James Callaghan, who would go on to be defeated by Margaret Thatcher and the Conservatives in 1979. Wilson remained in the Commons until 1979 before retiring to private life, spending much of his time at his favourite retreat, his astonishingly unassuming bungalow in the Isles of Scilly.

Wilson had married Gladys Mary Baldwin in 1939, and they had two sons. He was created Knight of the Garter in 1976 and was created a peer in 1983 as Lord Wilson of Rievaulx. He died in 1995. A memorial service was held in Westminster Abbey and he was buried in the churchyard cemetery at St Mary's Old Church in the Scilly Isles.

A statue of Harold Wilson in the city of his birth, Huddersfield. Unveiled in 1999 by another election-winning Labour Prime Minister, Tony Blair, the statue is notable for not featuring Wilson's trademark pipe.

EDWARD HEATH

Born:	9 July 1916
Died:	17 July 2005
Party:	Conservative
Served:	19 June 1970 – 4 March 1974
	(3 years, 259 days)

"I am not a product of privilege. I am a product of opportunity"

As PRIME MINISTER, Edward Heath led the United Kingdom into the European Community. His pro-European stance on domestic and foreign policy became one of the fault lines that would define Conservative Party debate for the ensuing decades, and his bitter opposition to Margaret Thatcher's policies of the 1980s and 1990s became a symbol of Conservative Party division.

Edward 'Ted' Heath was born of modest beginnings in Broadstairs, Kent, the son of William and Edith (*née* Pantony) Heath. His father was a carpenter who, through savings and grants, made sure that his son received an Oxford education. Indeed, Ted Heath was not only a fine student, but an outstanding musician as well, a quality that would be a large part of his personality for the rest of his life. He carried classical sheet music among his government papers wherever he travelled, and frequently would play at any available piano or organ for relaxation. His command of music was deep enough to enable him to conduct Elgar's *Cockaigne Overture* at London's Royal Festival Hall.

Before the Second World War, Heath was supporting Conservative Party candidates who voiced opposition to the policy of appeasement symbolised by the infamous Munich Agreement of 1938. Serving in the army during the war, he rose to the rank of colonel in the Royal Artillery. After 1945 Heath entered politics and was elected to Parliament in 1950. During the 1950s and 1960s Heath served under Conservative Party Prime Ministers in various Cabinet positions and by 1965 he had become Leader of the Opposition. Thus, upon victory in the general election of 1970, he became Prime Minister.

Heath sought to institute reforms in taxation, welfare, industrial relations, and government structure, but all of these programmes were secondary to Heath's vision of Britain joining the European Economic Community. He was sincerely convinced that Britain's future and her economic health were tied to full integration with her continental counterparts. To this end he worked assiduously and ultimately successfully, securing the Treaty of Accession in 1971 that brought the UK into Europe.

Heath's domestic policies ran into serious difficulties with the state of the economy and Northern Ireland. Inflation soared to nearly 20 per cent, while the price of energy, not yet benefiting from North Sea oil, skyrocketed. When coal miners went on strike it signalled a challenge to the Heath administration's ability to effectively govern and an election was called to settle the question. Meanwhile the 'Troubles' in Northern Ireland were also spiralling out of control. In June of 1972, fatalities resulted from the violence that erupted between British soldiers and Catholic marchers. These 'Bloody Sunday' deaths ushered in direct rule from London and a constant stream of terrorist actions that would plague the nation for decades.

The 1974 general elections saw a narrow defeat for Heath and the Conservative Party as Harold Wilson and the Labour Party returned to office. Heath's party leadership was also soon to end when Margaret Thatcher and a new Conservative philosophy arrived to not only replace Heath as party leader, but also begin a dramatic and revolutionary shift in British politics.

Heath stayed on in Parliament but never regained leadership of the Conservatives. Instead, he became the voice of Conservative protest against the Thatcher administration. He had no use for any part of Thatcherism, especially its distancing Britain from Europe and its controversial economic reforms. Politically, Heath became increasingly isolated, but he garnered respect for his conscience and later he became Father of the House of Commons.

Besides his great love of music, Heath was a notable sailor and participated in numerous international yachting events, winning the Sydney to Hobart race in 1969. Heath remained a lifelong bachelor and implied that a man could devote his life to government or his wife, but not both. In 1992 he was created a Knight of the Garter by Elizabeth II. He died in 2005 and is buried in Salisbury Cathedral. His former residence is just across the street from the great cathedral and is maintained for visits.

JAMES CALLAGHAN

Born:	27 March 1912
Died:	26 March 2005
Party:	Labour
Served:	5 April 1976 – 4 May 1979
	(3 years, 29 days)

*"A leader has to 'appear' consistent.
That doesn't mean he has
to be consistent"*

JAMES 'JIM' CALLAGHAN became Prime Minister following the sudden and unexpected resignation of Harold Wilson in April 1976. His term of office was turbulent and plagued by deep philosophical divisions within the Labour Party. Meanwhile, Britain was plagued by a host of economic problems, including sky-high inflation, crushing interest rates, and a general malaise of public confidence brought on by a seemingly endless parade of labour disputes and strikes. The winter of 1978/79 was labelled the 'Winter of Discontent' with the Callaghan government suffering numerous defeats in Parliament. The spring election of 1979 saw Callaghan's administration bearing the brunt of the discontent and the Labour Party being defeated by Margaret Thatcher and the Conservatives, who would go on to dominate Britain's politics for nearly the next two decades.

Leonard James Callaghan was born in Portsmouth, Hampshire, to James and Charlotte (*née* Cundy) Callaghan. His father died when he was young so, lacking a university education, Callaghan went to work as a tax clerk, joined a union, and in 1938 married a teacher, Audrey Moulton. They had one son and two daughters. Callaghan joined the Royal Navy during the Second World War, serving in the intelligence branch. He was elected to Parliament in 1945 as a Labour Party candidate for the seat of South Cardiff. Working his way through many union, Labour Party, and government posts, Callaghan became the only Prime Minister to have previously held the three major offices of state in the Cabinet: Chancellor of the Exchequer (1964–67), Home Secretary (1967–70), and Foreign Secretary (1974–76).

Nicknamed 'Sunny Jim' or 'Big Jim', Callaghan with Harold Wilson fought to keep the differing factions of the Labour Party together throughout the 1970s. Callaghan's forceful debating style, his ability to communicate on television, and his overall personality lent stability to his administration in the face of high unemployment, soaring inflation, and intractable relations with the trade unions. 'Sunny Jim' always felt that he could negotiate a common-ground position among the philosophical and practical differences within the various elements of his party and the more intransigent trade unions. In pursuit of his aims, 'Steady as she goes' became his frequent and optimistic refrain.

In foreign affairs, Callaghan played a major role in helping US President Jimmy Carter conclude the Camp David peace accord between Egypt and Israel. He negotiated the replacement of the submarine-launched Polaris missiles for the Royal Navy in defiance of heavy criticism – most of it from the extreme left of his own party. He did not flinch on standing up to the Soviet Union during the Cold War and got along well with American diplomat Henry Kissinger and US Presidents Ford and Carter.

Callaghan's defeat to Margaret Thatcher and the Conservatives in 1979 would lead to nearly twenty years of Tory government and the dismantling of many of the nationalised industries established by Labour after the Second World War. It would also mean the emasculation of the powerful trade unions and their stranglehold on many parts of the British economy. Callaghan had foreseen this possibility and had attempted to prevent it by controlling the leftward shift of the Labour Party. But the drift continued, and it was not until 1997, and Tony Blair's 'New Labour' appeal to the voters of 'middle of the road moderation', that the political pendulum would swing back in Labour's direction.

'Big Jim' Callaghan became Father of the House of Commons in 1983 and retired from Parliament in 1987, when he became Lord Callaghan of Cardiff. He died in 2005, was cremated, and his ashes were scattered over several locations, one being the site of the Peter Pan statue at London's Great Ormond Street Hospital for Children. Callaghan had been instrumental in renewing the hospital's claim to the royalties of *Peter Pan* that J. M. Barrie had donated in 1929. A plaque commemorates Callaghan's efforts.

Callaghan, as Prime Minister in 1978, chats to his predecessor Harold Wilson at an event to mark the 50th anniversary of all women getting the vote. They are ignoring Margaret Thatcher at their peril: she would go on to oust Callaghan in the following year's general election.

MARGARET THATCHER

Born: 13 October 1925
Party: Conservative
Served: 4 May 1979 – 28 November 1990
           (11 years, 209 days)

> *"I don't mind how much my ministers talk, as long as they do what I say"*

MARGARET THATCHER was the United Kingdom's first female Prime Minister, and also one of its most controversial. Few Prime Ministers have generated such emotional responses as Thatcher, and few have had such an enormous impact upon British history. She was the longest-serving twentieth-century PM, and her policies and stewardship created seismic shifts in social, economic, and individual behaviour and attitudes. Whatever one feels about Mrs Thatcher, her imprint cannot be denied, ignored, or overlooked.

She was born Margaret Hilda Roberts, in Grantham, Lincolnshire, the younger daughter of Alfred and Beatrice (*née* Stephenson) Roberts. Her father was a grocer and Margaret was brought up on conservative middle-class values of discipline and hard work. She attended the local Grantham grammar school before going on to Oxford to become a research chemist. She later returned to college in order to study law and qualify as a barrister. In 1951 she married a successful businessman, Denis Thatcher, with whom she had two children, a daughter and a son.

Mrs Thatcher entered Parliament in 1959 and became Secretary of State for Education and Science in 1970 under Prime Minister Edward Heath. Following the Conservative defeat in 1974, Thatcher replaced Heath as leader of the party in opposition. Thatcher then led the Conservatives to victory over the Labour Party in the 1979 general election and became Prime Minster, a post she would hold until 1990 – the longest continuous premiership since Robert Jenkinson (Lord Liverpool) during the Napoleonic Wars.

Thatcher set about restructuring much of the British economy and its social underpinnings through the privatisation of government-owned industries (oil, gas, telecommunications, transportation, heavy industry, etc.) dating back to the post-war Attlee administration. She also sought to lower taxes, reduce inflation, and take on the powerful trade unions to reduce their influence and grip on industry. Her confrontation with the coal miners in 1984 proved to Britain, the trade unions, and the Labour Party that it would no longer be business as usual. There would be no backing down, no concessions or compromise by her government. When Thatcher emerged triumphant, it was clear to all that a new relationship between British business, industry, and labour now existed. The political and social hold of the trade unions had been convincingly broken.

In foreign affairs, Margaret Thatcher put her reputation on the line in the Falklands War with Argentina, and again emerged victorious. Arm in arm with President Ronald Reagan, she was a strident Cold War warrior, challenging the Soviet Union in frank and direct terms, being duly dubbed the 'Iron Lady' by the Soviets. She maintained the UK's nuclear deterrent by modernising the submarine fleet with the advanced Trident missile, but she also welcomed the proposed reforms of Soviet leader Mikhail Gorbachev. Thatcher, Reagan and the West would rejoice in the fall of the Berlin Wall in 1989 and celebrate the ensuing collapse of the Soviet Union.

She won general election victories in 1983 and again in 1987, while surviving an IRA assassination attempt in 1984 (in which an explosion in a Brighton hotel killed five and narrowly missed killing her). She was reluctant to fully embrace participation in Europe and this led to major divisions in Cabinet and the Conservative Party. Her domestic plan to reform local government charges was dubbed a 'Poll Tax' and met with stiff resistance; by 1990 her seeming invincibility had been considerably eroded. She was challenged for the party leadership in 1990 and resigned after failing to win the contest outright. She was replaced by her Chancellor of the Exchequer, John Major.

Margaret Thatcher remained in the Commons until retiring in 1992, when she was created Baroness Thatcher of Kesteven. Her husband Denis died in 2003. Though certainly controversial, her undeniably enormous impact and legacy are evident across the modern political and social landscape of the United Kingdom.

Margaret Thatcher and Ronald Reagan meet for talks in the White House in 1981. They greatly admired each other, and both survived assassination attempts.

JOHN MAJOR

Born:	29 March 1943
Party:	Conservative
Served:	28 November 1990 – 2 May 1997
	(6 years, 154 days)

"The politician who never makes a mistake never made a decision"

JOHN MAJOR came from a humble background, growing up in the Brixton area of London and leaving school at sixteen without an opportunity for a university education. Unemployed and looking after his ill and elderly parents, Major joined the Brixton branch of the Young Conservatives, became a bank clerk, and through hard work, determination, and not a little good fortune, climbed the ladder of parliamentary politics. He became Prime Minister in 1990, replacing Margaret Thatcher, and against long odds won a Conservative electoral victory in 1992 that kept him and his party in power until 1997.

Major was the son of Thomas and Gwendolyn (*née* Coates) Major, both with backgrounds in the theatre. His father, also known as Abraham Thomas Ball, had been a bricklayer, acrobat, juggler, and theatre comedian. Major's banking career and early political positions were all modest and unspectacular. He was married in 1970 to a schoolteacher, Norma Johnson. He was elected to Parliament on his third attempt in 1979, whereupon he began a rapid rise through the ranks of the Tories, culminating in his appointments under Margaret Thatcher as Foreign Secretary in 1987 and Chancellor of the Exchequer in 1989. It was at this time that Thatcher's popularity and power within the Conservative Party were beginning to seriously wane, opening the door for Major to emerge as a potential successor.

When Thatcher lost the confidence of her party, she supported Major over other Cabinet members such as Michael Heseltine and Douglas Hurd. Major was viewed as a fresh face and an opportunity for the Conservatives to shed the negative images that some of Thatcher's policies had generated. The decision turned out to be a wise one, and after the spectacularly successful first Gulf War (1990–91) Major's popularity rose. His basic and personable 'soap box' campaign across the UK in 1992 brought about a surprise electoral victory when defeat had been widely predicted.

However, Major's next five years were a struggle. Economic recession, political scandals, and a division within the nation and the Conservative Party over the contentious issue of how deeply Britain should align with the European Union, all led to a crushing electoral defeat in 1997. After nearly two decades of Conservative government, Britain was ready for change; Tony Blair's 'New' Labour Party provided it to the tune of a 179-seat majority in Parliament – the worst defeat for the Conservatives since Arthur Balfour's trouncing in 1906.

After the defeat, Major immediately resigned his position as party leader. He left Parliament and politics altogether in 2001. He has remained in the public eye by making frequent appearances as a guest speaker, though he turned down an invitation by the Conservative Party to run for Mayor of London in 2008. In 2005, Major was created a Knight of the Garter by Queen Elizabeth II.

Major has been criticised for not leading more strongly or offering a bolder vision; but he always proclaimed himself to be a practical man, a politician willing and able to achieve compromise and results. His successful negotiations over the Maastricht Treaty concerning the European Union brought benefit to the UK, and his work in the endlessly difficult negotiations concerning Northern Ireland laid the groundwork for a future power-sharing agreement between Protestants and Catholics.

A British reconaissance vehicle, sporting the Union Jack at its rear, enters Kuwait during Operation Desert Storm in February 1991. John Major's leadership in the first Gulf War was much more popular and less controversial than Tony Blair's role in the second.

TONY BLAIR

Born:	6 May 1953
Party:	Labour
Served:	2 May 1997 – 27 June 2007
	(10 years, 56 days)

*"Do I know I'm right? Judgements
aren't the same as facts. Instinct
is not science. I'm like any other
human being, as fallible and as
capable of being wrong. I only
know what I believe"*

TONY BLAIR became Prime Minister of the United Kingdom in 1997, leading his 'New' Labour Party to an overwhelming victory and returning a Labour Prime Minster to power for the first time since 1979. Blair would then remain in office for a decade, winning two further general elections. In 2007 he turned over the leadership of his party and the country to Gordon Brown, his Chancellor of the Exchequer. Blair's dynamic personality, brilliance in debate, and skill in modern campaigning had led Labour to three resounding electoral victories and forged an entirely new image of his party.

Tony Blair was born in Edinburgh, Scotland, the second son of Leo and Hazel (*née* Corscaden) Blair. Educated at St John's College, Oxford, Blair entered Parliament in 1983. At university he enjoyed acting in the theatre, playing guitar, and singing in a rock band called Ugly Rumours. Blair moved to London, became a lawyer, and met his wife, Cherie Booth, also a lawyer. They were married in 1980 and went on to have four children. Together they became involved in the Labour Party, a party that was attempting to redefine itself under the leadership of Neil Kinnock and, later, John Smith (who was to suddenly die of a heart attack in 1994). Upon Smith's death, Blair inherited the leadership of the party in opposition, a position that showcased his brilliance in parliamentary debate. It also placed him in charge of organising the campaign for the next general election, and became an opportunity to display his election team's genius for conveying a message of 'change'.

The 'New Labour' movement was rooted in several policy changes and promises: friendliness to business and the free market as engineered by Blair's Chancellor, Gordon Brown; a clear break and distancing from the 'hard' left extremism of the Tony

Benn wing of the party; and a reduction of the influence of trade unions, long a pillar of traditional Labour strength. The national shift in political mood and social attitude, reflected in repeated Conservative Party election victories, was not lost on the Young Turks in the Labour Party, and after nearly two decades of Thatcher and Major, the country was ready for a change. Blair and his cohorts made sure that New Labour was ready to seize the opportunity for change that presented itself at the general election of May 1997. They were not disappointed. Labour won conclusively, with Tony Blair going on to become the party's longest-serving Prime Minister and the only Labour PM to win three consecutive elections.

Blair and the Labour Party moved quickly on several political fronts. The promise of devolution (a degree of self-government) for Wales and Scotland was promptly secured. The Good Friday Agreement between Unionists and Nationalists, tempering the age-old conflict between Protestants and Catholics, seemed to have quelled the troubles in Northern Ireland. And the intervention by British and US military forces in the former Yugoslavia successfully brought about peace and order. Blair also fully supported and accompanied the US invasion of Afghanistan in 2001, seeking to remove the terrorist threat of al-Qaida.

These apparent successes, however, were to be contrasted with the heavy criticism Blair endured during the run-up to the second Gulf War in 2003, in which Blair supported the invasion of Iraq by US and British forces in order to remove Saddam Hussein from power.

The terrorist attacks in the US on 11 September 2001 and later the London terrorist bombings of 7 July 2005 had critically changed the political landscape and raised serious questions about how best to fight the threat of terrorism. Blair's firm stance in relation to this threat invited admiration from some but opposition from others who believed civil liberties were being threatened by the government's actions. There is ongoing controversy over Blair's legacy with regard to the war in Iraq and his government's raft of new legislation to counter terrorism.

Blair resigned as leader of the Labour Party and Prime Minister in June 2007 following reported friction between him and his purported successor and erstwhile close associate Gordon Brown. Blair has since spent much time as a UN peace envoy in the Middle East. In December 2007, he joined the religion of his wife and became a Roman Catholic. He makes public appearances, gives speeches, and has been awarded with several honours around the world, but his critics are at least as numerous as his admirers.

GORDON BROWN

Born:	20 February 1951
Party:	Labour
Served:	27 June 2007 – 11 May 2010
	(2 years, 319 days)

"I remember words that have stayed with me since my childhood and which matter a great deal today: my school motto, 'I will try my utmost'. This is my promise to all of the people of Britain"

GORDON BROWN became Prime Minister of the United Kingdom in June 2007 upon the resignation of Tony Blair. Blair had served as leader of the Labour Party since 1994 and as Prime Minister since 1997, with Brown serving as Chancellor of the Exchequer during Blair's years as PM. Many speculated that they had not only agreed to work in concert, but that if the Labour Party continued in power, Blair would eventually step down and hand over the reins to Brown.

Gordon Brown was born in 1951 near Glasgow, Scotland, the son of John and Jessie Elizabeth (*née* Souter) Brown. His father was a minister in the Church of Scotland and his mother the daughter of a timber merchant. At the age of sixteen he was injured in a rugby match and lost the sight in one eye. He graduated from Edinburgh University and entered Parliament in 1983. Together with Tony Blair and other like-minded members of the Labour Party, he developed policies that were pro-business and friendly to the middle classes, giving birth to what was to be 'New Labour'. It was a huge success and brought Blair, Brown and their party to power.

Brown, as Prime Minister, by and large maintained policies introduced by Tony Blair. He supported the Afghanistan and Iraq invasions and remained committed to combating global terrorism, though admitting that mistakes were made in going to war in Iraq and that the policy toward fighting terrorism must be continually re-evaluated. Brown has received praise for stemming the potential banking collapse with a well-timed government infusion of badly needed capital. But he also earned a reputation for his lack of administration management skills due to his reportedly volatile hair-trigger temper.

The so-called 'Credit Crunch' – the economic downturn that affected the globe from 2008 – combined with a perceived malaise at the end of over a decade of Labour leadership would spell electoral defeat for Brown and Labour in the spring of 2010. Brown resigned in May 2010 and was replaced by the Conservative leader David Cameron, who formed a coalition government since he had not been able to achieve an outright majority in Parliament.

Gordon Brown married Sarah Macaulay in 2000, and their marriage has produced three children: a daughter (who died shortly after birth) and two sons.

Queen Elizabeth II has been on the throne of the United Kingdom since 1952. She has been served by thirteen Prime Ministers to date, the first being Winston Churchill.

DAVID CAMERON

Born:	9 October 1966
Party:	Conservative
Served:	11 May 2010 –

*"There is such a thing as society.
It's just not the same thing
as the state."*

DAVID CAMERON became Prime Minister following the general election of May 2010. His Conservative Party gained the most seats in the Commons but lacked an overall majority. To overcome this 'hung' Parliament, Cameron formed a coalition government with the Liberal Democrats, the first such coalition government since the Second World War. In return for Lib-Dem support, Cameron and the Conservatives agreed to several policy concessions and named Lib-Dem leader Nick Clegg as Deputy Prime Minister.

Cameron was born in London, the son of Ian and Mary (*née* Mount) Cameron. Though not of royal birth, he is a descendant of King William IV (1765–1837) and his mistress Dorothea Jordan. He was educated at Eton and Oxford before eventually becoming Director of Corporate Affairs at Carlton Communications, a media company. He was elected to Parliament in 2001 and quickly rose through the ranks of the Conservative Party, becoming party leader in 2005, promising to change the party's fortunes and return it to power after three successive election defeats.

Cameron married Samantha Gwendoline Sheffield in 1996. The marriage has produced four children, two boys and two girls; their eldest son, Ivan, died in 2009 at the age of six.

At forty-three, Cameron became the youngest Prime Minister since Robert Jenkinson (Lord Liverpool) assumed the post in 1812 at the age of forty-two during the Napoleonic Wars.

DATES OF SERVICE

1721–1742	Sir Robert Walpole
1742–1743	Earl of Wilmington
1743–1754	Henry Pelham
1754–1756	Duke of Newcastle
1756–1757	Duke of Devonshire
1757–1762	Duke of Newcastle
1762–1763	Earl of Bute
1763–1765	George Grenville
1765–1766	Marquess of Rockingham
1766–1768	William Pitt the Elder
1768–1770	Duke of Grafton
1770–1782	Lord North
1782	Marquess of Rockingham
1782–1783	Earl of Shelburne
1783	Duke of Portland
1783–1801	William Pitt the Younger
1801–1804	Henry Addington
1804–1806	William Pitt the Younger
1806–1807	Lord William Grenville
1807–1809	Duke of Portland
1809–1812	Spencer Perceval
1812–1827	Earl of Liverpool
1827	George Canning
1827–1828	Viscount Goderich
1828–1830	Duke of Wellington
1830–1834	Earl Grey
1834	Viscount Melbourne
1834–1835	Sir Robert Peel
1835–1841	Viscount Melbourne
1841–1846	Sir Robert Peel
1846–1852	Lord John Russell
1852	Earl of Derby

1852–1855	Earl of Aberdeen
1855–1858	Viscount Palmerston
1858–1859	Earl of Derby
1859–1865	Viscount Palmerston
1865–1866	Earl Russell
1866–1868	Earl of Derby
1868	Benjamin Disraeli
1868–1874	William Gladstone
1874–1880	Benjamin Disraeli
1880–1885	William Gladstone
1885–1886	Marquess of Salisbury
1886	William Gladstone
1886–1892	Marquess of Salisbury
1892–1894	William Gladstone
1894–1895	Earl of Rosebery
1895–1902	Marquess of Salisbury
1902–1905	Arthur Balfour
1905–1908	Sir Henry Campbell-Bannerman
1908–1916	Herbert Asquith
1916–1922	David Lloyd George
1922–1923	Andrew Bonar Law
1923–1924	Stanley Baldwin
1924	James Ramsay MacDonald
1924–1929	Stanley Baldwin
1929–1935	James Ramsay MacDonald
1935–1937	Stanley Baldwin
1937–1940	Neville Chamberlain
1940–1945	Winston Churchill
1945–1951	Clement Attlee
1951–1955	Sir Winston Churchill
1955–1957	Sir Anthony Eden
1957–1963	Harold Macmillan
1963–1964	Sir Alec Douglas-Home
1964–1970	Harold Wilson
1970–1974	Edward Heath
1974–1976	Harold Wilson
1976–1979	James Callaghan
1979–1990	Margaret Thatcher
1990–1997	John Major
1997–2007	Tony Blair
2007–2010	Gordon Brown
2010–	David Cameron

LIST OF MONARCHS

	Reigned
George I	1714–1727
George II	1727–1760
George III	1760–1820
George IV	1820–1830
William IV	1830–1837
Victoria	1837–1901
Edward VII	1901–1910
George V	1910–1936
Edward VIII	1936
George VI	1936–1952
Elizabeth II	1952–

PICTURE CREDITS

While every effort has been made to trace the copyright holders for illustrations featured in this book, the publishers will be glad to make proper acknowledgements in future editions in the event that any regrettable omissions have occurred at the time of going to press.

Images on pages 13, 34, 36, 40, 71 and 97 courtesy of the Library of Congress.

Images on pages 73, 75, 77, 81, 85, 87, 89, 91 and 93 courtesy of the Library of Congress / George Bain Collection.

Images on pages 109, 111, 115, 117, 119 and 121 courtesy of the U.S. Government.

Images on pages 55 and 63 courtesy of The London Library.

Images on pages 17, 19, 21, 25, 29, 32, 38, 43, 45, 47, 49, 51, 53, 65, 67, 69, 95, 107 and 113 courtesy of Mary Evans Picture Library.

Images on pages 79, 83, 100 and 103 courtesy of Mary Evans Picture Library / Illustrated London News Ltd.

Image on page 105 courtesy of Mary Evans Picture Library / Roger Mayne.

Images on pages 15, 16, 18, 22, 23, 27, 31, 35, 41, 42, 46, 48, 52, 54, 57, 59, 60, 62, 64, 66, 70, 80, 84, 88, 90, 99, 102, 104, 106, 108, 110, 114, 116, 118, 122 and 123 are in the public domain.

ACKNOWLEDGEMENTS

A short note of thanks is necessary for those who encouraged me in this project, from my dearest English cousins to the numerous townsfolk throughout the UK who were uniformly friendly and helpful to me in my researching of the various prime ministerial sites. A big thank you to the crew at Amberley Publishing: to Sarah Flight for her initial response; to Alan Sutton for his faith and belief in the book; and of course to my hardworking project editor Robert Drew, whose suggestions, comments and support were invaluable. Lastly and most importantly, I dedicate this book to my wife Sheila and our son Robbie, who displayed endless patience and support while accompanying me on various trips to the UK as we visited a myriad of churches, graveyards, cathedrals, manor houses and museums in search of accurately identifying every prime ministerial burial site. Any errors of fact or interpretation in this book are mine alone.

R. J. P.